GREAT MYSTERIES

Voodoo

OPPOSING VIEWPOINTS®

Look for these and other exciting *Great Mysteries:*
Opposing Viewpoints books:

GREAT MYSTERIES

Voodoo

OPPOSING VIEWPOINTS®

by Don Nardo
and Erik Belgum

Greenhaven Press, Inc.   P.O. Box 289009, San Diego, California 92198-0009

Library of Congress Cataloging-in-Publication Data

Nardo, Don 1947-
  Voodoo : opposing viewpoints / Don Nardo and Erik Belgum
    p. cm. — (Great mysteries)
  Includes bibliographical references and index.
  ISBN 0-89908-089-8
  1. Voodooism — Juvenile literature. 2. Santeria (Cultus) —Juvenile
  literature. 3. Hoodoo (Cult) — Juvenile literature. I. Nardo, Don,
  1947-   . II. Title. III. Series: Great mysteries.
  BL2490.B37 1991
  299'.67—dc20   91-14497
                                                                   CIP
                                                                    AC

Contents

Introduction

This book is written for the curious—those who want to explore the mysteries that are everywhere. To be human is to be constantly surrounded by wonderment. How do birds fly? Are ghosts real? Can animals and people communicate? Was King Arthur a real person or a myth? Why did Amelia Earhart disappear? Did history really happen the way we think it did? Where did the world come from? Where is it going?

Great Mysteries: Opposing Viewpoints books are intended to offer the reader an opportunity to explore some of the many mysteries that both trouble and intrigue us. For the span of each book, we want the reader to feel that he or she is a scientist investigating the extinction of the dinosaurs, an archaeologist searching for clues to the origin of the great Egyptian pyramids, a psychic detective testing the existence of ESP.

One thing all mysteries have in common is that there is no ready answer. Often there are *many* answers but none on which even the majority of authorities agrees. *Great Mysteries: Opposing Viewpoints* books introduce the intriguing views of the experts, allowing the reader to participate in their explorations, their theories, and their disagreements as they try to explain the mysteries of our world.

But most readers won't want to stop here. These *Great Mysteries: Opposing Viewpoints* aim to stimulate the reader's curiosity. Although truth is often impossible to discover, the search is fascinating. It is up to the reader to examine the evidence, to decide whether the answer is there—or to explore further.

"Penetrating so many secrets, we cease to believe in the unknowable. But there it sits nevertheless, calmly licking its chops."

H.L. Mencken, American essayist

Prologue

A Strange and Powerful Spectacle

Wade Davis, a young graduate student from Harvard University, carefully climbed to the summit of a hill overlooking the sea. He watched the setting sun cast long, distinct shadows across the fields and mountains of the exotic island. He had journeyed to this mysterious land in order to witness a ceremony few foreigners had ever seen. Slowly, he entered a fenced-in terrace in front of a small building that the islanders called a temple. A crowd of about thirty people, some islanders and some foreigners, sat at tables facing the entrance to the temple. Three male islanders sat quietly behind large drums, the men and instruments illuminated by a fire in a hearth and by small lanterns hung on poles. Most of the visitors seemed quietly excited, anticipating the events to come.

As Davis took his seat, a female priest appeared. She was a tall black woman carrying a clay jar and a container of water. She was followed by a young woman dressed in a white robe. The young woman placed a candle on the ground and lit it, after which the priest knelt and opened the clay jar. The onlookers silently watched as she removed cornmeal from the jar and began tracing designs in the dirt. Next, the priest poured water from the con-

These African-style drums used at Voodoo ceremonies create the entrancing rhythms that help Voodoo dancers alter their state of consciousness.

tainer into the dirt near the designs she had made. She then repeated this gesture in front of each drum. Several more robed figures appeared, and the priest guided them into a circle. A male priest now emerged from the temple. He was heavyset and had a solemn expression on his face. After the figures knelt, he began to pray out loud in a strange, ancient language. For several minutes, only the sound of his deep, resonant voice echoed across the hilltop.

Then the drummers began pounding. Each drum had a different sound and a different rhythm, yet the three seemed to blend into one powerful, compelling force. Suddenly, the robed figures were on their feet and dancing. Their feet traced simple steps in the dirt, but their heads and arms and shoulders swung wildly. There was a primitive energy to the dancing, an energy that seemed to flow up from the earth, into the drums, and finally into the dancers themselves. For more than thirty minutes, the dancers continued, never once resting, never so much as breaking their concentration. And all the while, the two priests prayed, invoking the names of ancient and mysterious spirits.

Possession

Then, without warning, one of the dancers froze, and the drumbeats changed. The dancer spun around on one foot, then hurled herself through the air. She fell to the ground, gasping, slicing the air with her arms and legs. The visitors, tense with excitement, leaned forward for a better look. As they did so, the dancer suddenly ceased her spasms and slowly rose to her feet. According to island belief, a spirit was now in possession of her body. She swiftly made her way around the terrace, as if searching for something. Looks of surprise and shock came over the faces of the visitors as she easily lifted a man twice her size high into the air. Dropping him, she seized a glass from one of the tables. She bit into it, and the audience gasped. The visitors watched closely as she spit the broken fragments across the terrace. They were amazed that there was no blood. Next, the woman priest presented the dancer with a live bird. The young woman immediately broke its wings and tore its neck apart with her teeth.

For several more minutes, the wild dance continued. Another dancer became possessed. She grasped hot coals from the fire in each hand, then placed another in her mouth and danced on. Finally, she collapsed into the arms of the female priest, who removed the coals. The dancer had not been burned. The islanders claimed that this was because the spirit inhabiting her body was immune to the effects of fire.

Eventually, the dancers became themselves again, and the drums stopped. The robed figures slowly retreated back into the temple, while the male priest walked over and greeted Davis. He told the priest that the spectacle had been both exciting and surprising. He admitted he was not sure if the dancers had really been possessed by spirits, but it had certainly seemed as if they were. Davis was unable to explain how the dancers showed such great physical strength and avoided being cut or burned. He had come to the island of Haiti to see a real Voodoo ceremony, and he had not been disappointed.

One

Out of Africa

Voodoo is the religion practiced by most of the inhabitants of Haiti, an island country in the Caribbean Sea. The natives of Haiti refer to the faith as Vodoun, a word that comes from an African word for "spirit." A number of other faiths developed from or had the same roots as Voodoo. One of these is Santeria, which was originally practiced in Cuba and later spread to parts of the United States. Other examples are Shango, practiced on the island of Trinidad, Obeah, practiced on the island of Jamaica, and Candomblé, practiced in Brazil.

Voodoo is one of the most misunderstood of all the world's religions. Many people of other faiths associate Voodoo primarily with black magic, witchcraft, evil spirits, and the walking dead. Although some of these phenomena occasionally play a role in Voodoo, they are not the major aspects of the faith.

Like all religions, Voodoo has some supernatural elements, including evil ones. But most aspects of Voodoo are positive and fulfilling for those who practice the faith. Nevertheless, many of the practices involved in Voodoo remain mysterious and awesome, even for believers. This book will examine Voodoo's origins, beliefs, and practices, espe-

14

cially in Haiti, where more people practice the faith than in any other place. The book will dispel popular myths about Voodoo and explore the real mysteries surrounding this strange and unique faith.

From the Mists of Time

Voodoo and its offshoots have their roots in the religions of western Africa, particularly the area now occupied by the countries of Nigeria, Benin, and Togo. This was and still is the home of the

African religious rituals included dancing oneself into a trance. Voodoo believers continue this practice today.

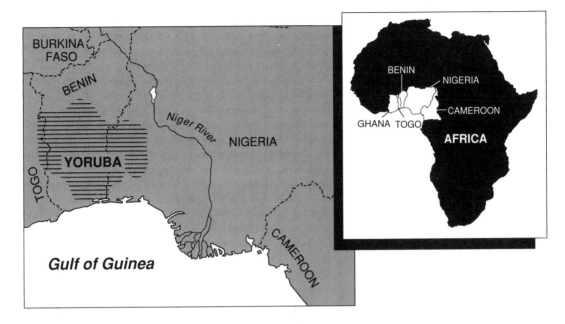

Yoruba people. During the sixteenth, seventeenth, and eighteenth centuries, French and Spanish slave traders raided Yoruba lands. The white raiders captured many of the Yoruba and transported them to Haiti and other Caribbean islands. There the slaves privately carried on many of the religious traditions of their native Africa. Over the course of time, these beliefs changed somewhat as the people adapted to the new ideas and customs that were forced upon them. A new faith developed, the one now referred to as Voodoo. Yet many of its basic tenets, or principles, remained those of the Yoruba.

The Yoruba have lived in Africa for at least twenty-five hundred years, and the origins of their faith are rooted deep in time. According to Yoruba tradition, there is one high god, the Gran Mèt, or Grand Master. His name is Olorun, and he rules the universe. Originally, there were also a few less powerful gods, among them Obatala and Oduduwa. The Yoruba faith holds that long ago, Olorun gave permission to Obatala to create the earth and human

This map of Africa shows the territory of the Yoruba. European slave traders raided these lands and carried off their inhabitants to work on New World plantations. In their harsh, new surroundings, the slaves had to practice their native religion secretly.

beings. But Oduduwa stole this privilege and began creation on his own. There followed a battle between Oduduwa and Obatala. It ended in Obatala's defeat and banishment. Later, Oduduwa had a change of heart and invited Obatala to return and join him in watching over the earth in peace. The people rejoiced at Obatala's return, and today many Yoruba continue to hold an annual festival celebrating the event. Thus Yoruba myths, like those of many other religions, hold that the earth was created during a period of chaos and violence, followed by the promise of eternal peace.

The Yoruba religion pays respect to about four hundred lesser spirits or saints called *orisa* (or *orisha*). The Yoruba believe these spirits were once humans who led extremely good or heroic lives.

African worshipers dance and chant in hopes that they can influence the spirits to intercede in earthly affairs.

When they died, the Gran Mèt made them immortal so that they would remain as examples to people of future generations. The orisa can be compared to the saints of Christianity, humans who achieved immortality through good deeds or sacrifice. Each orisa has a specific duty or special quality that sets him or her apart from all the others. For example, Sango, the spirit of thunder, controls the movement of storms. (Shango is another name for this spirit, who became one of the main deities in the religion on the island of Trinidad.) Another Yoruba orisa, Osun, is the spirit who creates and watches over streams that have medicinal, or healing, properties. Oko is the spirit of farming, and Erinle is the deity who rules over the forests.

The most important of all the orisa is Ogun, the god of iron, hunting, war, and warriors. Worship of Ogun is more widespread among the Yoruba than the worship of any other orisa. This is because the Yoruba recognize in Ogun one of the great, and at the same time sad, truths of life. Ogun shows humans that violence, although destructive, is a necessary part of life. For example, people must kill either plants or animals to live. People must strive to be nonviolent, but they always face the danger that violence will become all-consuming, destroying not only themselves but also their loved ones. In Ogun, the Yoruba see a reflection of themselves. Ogun is usually strong and good, but sometimes he can lose control and hurt the ones he loves.

Yoruba Rituals

The Yoruba's worship of the Gran Mèt and the orisas is similar to worship in most other religions: Through prayers and religious ceremonies, believers seek to establish contact with God or the gods. Worshipers hope they can influence the spirits to intercede in human or other earthly affairs. The Yoruba try to influence the spirits by offering gifts, which take several forms. One gift is prayer. People

"'Voodoo' is a religion which inspires horror in most Americans, but explained by one of its own priests it seems no more formidable than Presbyterianism."

Charles Alva Hoyt, *Witchcraft*

"Presbyterians and other mainstream Christians are not likely to practice animal sacrifice, engage in divination with shells or palm nuts, succumb to trance possession, cast spells, or worship the serpent god Damballah-wèdo or other such *loa*."

Dean Peerman, *The Christian Century*, July 16-23, 1986

18

can either pray individually or in a formal ceremony presided over by a priest called *babalawo*, or "father of ancient wisdom."

Another Yoruba gift to the gods is the sacrifice of an animal. Almost every Yoruba ceremony involves the ritual slaughter of an animal, usually a goat, sheep, or dog. Such sacrifices serve several purposes. First, they acknowledge that life and death are intertwined, that death always follows life. Second, sacrificed animals are thought to be food for the orisa. Since each orisa, like each person, has different desires and tastes, a specific sacrifice is appropriate for each spirit. For example, Ogun, who presides over the hunt, receives the sacrifice of a dog, an animal that often assists in hunting. Another reason for ritual sacrifice is to gain the favor of a particular spirit who might then help the bearer of the sacrifice. In this way, the Yoruba believe, it is possible to temporarily ward off such ills as death, disease, famine, or poverty.

These and other religious beliefs were the glue that held the early western African societies together. The people were hunters, gatherers, and farmers, who depended upon the land for their livings. The spirits were an integral part of nature and determined whether the land would be bountiful. A good relationship between the people and the spirits was essential. People strove to maintain a balance in which they led good lives and sacrificed to the spirits; the spirits in turn provided good harvests, health, and luck. To these Africans, religious faith was as much a part of life as eating and breathing were.

A Life of Misery

Faith remained important to the thousands of Africans who came to the New World in chains in the 1600s and 1700s. They tried to carry on the religious beliefs and customs that had been an essential part of their lives. But practicing the old ways was

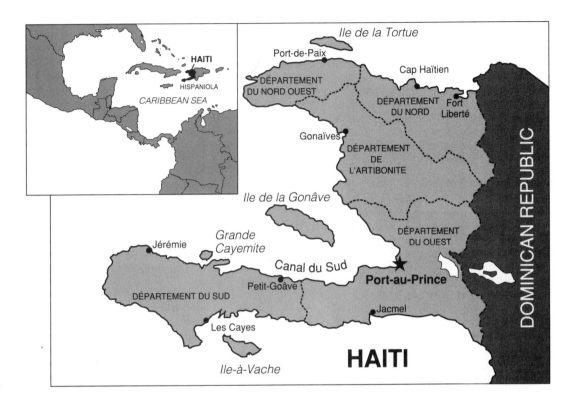

difficult because their lives were no longer the same. Their entire existence now revolved around doing the bidding of their white masters. The slave owners frowned on and tried to suppress customs that connected the slaves to their old lives.

In Haiti, then called Saint Domingue, life for the slaves was incredibly harsh. They worked in the fields all day and every day, tending and harvesting crops. Among these were cotton, coffee, tobacco, and sugarcane. At that time, Saint Domingue's supplies of these commodities were very important to France. In fact, the island provided two-thirds of all French overseas trade and was considered the most valuable colony in the world. To keep this precious pipeline of crops flowing across the ocean, the French depended on the labor of countless slaves. In the 1780s, there were more than 500,000 black slaves in Saint Domingue, dominated by a mere 35,000 white planters. To ensure productivity, the planters drove the slaves hard, giving them little time to rest. Overseers brutally whipped those who did not work fast enough. Often, field hands were forced to work in the hot tropical sun until they fainted or died from exhaustion.

To make sure the slaves did not break rules or try to run away, the planters imposed cruel punishments. For example, slaves who ran away and were recaptured often had their leg muscles sliced. Those who broke even minor rules were sometimes hung from nails driven through their ears. Some planters cut off the ears of rule breakers or whipped them until the bones were exposed. Other common punishments included dipping body parts in boiling cane syrup, mutilating the sex organs, and burning

A slave driver on Saint Domingue takes a whip from his belt to flog a slave. White slaveholders used cruel and regular punishment to intimidate their slaves and keep them submissive.

out the eyes with red-hot irons. Often, slave owners killed slaves to set an example and strike fear in the hearts of other slaves. This practice was so widespread that some Frenchmen in Saint Domingue made their livings as professional executioners. Their fees were set by law. For instance, it cost thirty pounds to hang a slave and five pounds to cut off his or her ears.

Something to Cling to

Living under such miserable and cruel conditions, the slaves had nothing to look forward to in life. Some committed suicide rather than endure such hardships. Some women gave themselves abortions to keep their children from being born into slavery. For the vast majority of slaves, the only comfort was in remembering the old life in Africa. Most clung to the worship of the traditional spirits as a way of giving meaning to otherwise meaningless lives.

Memories of the old life of freedom in Africa continually remained strong among the slaves. New slaves from western Africa constantly arrived in Saint Domingue. And slave children born in the colony learned early that their parents had come from a better place far away. Africa itself became one of the major concepts of the Voodoo faith as it developed in the Caribbean. The slaves referred to Africa as Gine (Guinea), their ancestral home. In time, because the ocean separated the old world of the slaves from the new, Gine also became known as the undersea realm of many Voodoo spirits.

Many of the same spirits worshiped by the Yoruba and other inhabitants of western Africa remained important in Voodoo beliefs in Saint Domingue. But because social and economic conditions were different in the Caribbean, the roles, images, and even the names of many of these spirits changed. For instance, Ogun, the most widely worshiped of the Yoruba spirits, became Ogoun in Saint

"Some Haitian intellectuals denounce [Voodoo] as an opiate of the desperately poor Haitian masses."

Susan Katz, *Newsweek*, February 24, 1986

"The inner man also needs security; it's precisely because he is so poor and always in danger of want or illness that the peasant is strongly attached to voodoo."

Alfred Métraux, *Voodoo in Haiti*

Slaves tend the sugarcane crop on Saint Domingue. Slaves' religious beliefs helped them cope with their harsh and burdensome life.

Domingue. Ogun was associated with hunting and the smelting of metals such as iron, as well as with warfare. All of these activities played an important part in Yoruba society. But the slaves of the Caribbean had a very different way of life. They no longer hunted for a living. Nor did they produce iron artifacts. So, Ogoun became less associated with these things and more involved with aspects of life that the slaves could relate to. Believers in

Voodoo prayed to Ogoun, still the spirit of warriors, for the strength to withstand captivity and for the power to overthrow their masters.

A Merging of Faiths

Unfortunately, the slaves in Saint Domingue had to hide the practice of their African-based religion. As mentioned earlier, the white plantation owners frowned on any customs that tied the slaves to their previous lives. Also, the French slave masters were Catholic. They believed that theirs was the only true faith, and they viewed other religious beliefs as primitive and sacrilegious. They tried to suppress the slaves' beliefs and force them to practice Catholicism. Baptism into the Catholic church became mandatory for all slaves, and the slaves had to learn about Catholic ceremonies, customs, and saints.

But the slaves never actually gave up their own beliefs or completely converted to Catholicism. Instead, they merged some Christian ideas and images

This drawing depicts slaves secretly practicing Voodoo rituals. Sitting musicians and drummers provide rhythms for the dancers while the female high priest presides from her chair.

This drawing depicts Christ and his disciples at the Last Supper. At this ritual meal, Christ gave blessed bread and wine to his followers to eat, telling them it was his own flesh and blood. African slaves, forced to convert to Catholicism, thought the Christian ritual was similar to their own sacrificial rituals. They assimilated other Christian ideas into their religion as well.

with those of their African-based faith. They did this for two reasons. First, it allowed them to give the necessary appearance of practicing Catholicism while continuing to worship the traditional African spirits. Second, the slaves liked some aspects of Christianity and eagerly incorporated them into their own faith. Thus, Voodoo is a syncretic religion, one that is formed by uniting ideas from two or more faiths.

The slaves found it easy to merge their African faith with Catholicism because they saw many similarities between the two religions. Both recognize the existence of supernatural powers; both preach that there is life after death; both believe one high god rules the universe. In addition, both Catholicism and the Yoruba religion have ceremonies that revolve around blood sacrifices. The worshipers often ritually consume the flesh and blood of animals sacrificed to the orisas in ceremonies that they believe strengthen the relationship between human beings and the spirits. The Haitian slaves saw striking similarities in Catholic communion. In this ceremony, the worshipers ritually consume the flesh and blood of Jesus Christ. This ritual also serves to strengthen the relationship between Catholics and what they believe to be the Spirit of God.

Helping Spirits

Perhaps the most striking similarity between Christianity and the religion practiced by the Haitian slaves was the concept of helping spirits.

Christian worshipers drink blessed wine that symbolizes the sacrificial blood of Christ as a way of gaining spiritual nourishment from Christ. Voodoo practitioners believe they receive spiritual help and strength from their gods by partaking of ritual sacrifices.

Christian legend says that St. Patrick drove out the snakes from Ireland. Voodoo believers identify him with the West African snake god, Dambala.

The slaves called the spirits *loa*, which came from an old Yoruba word meaning "mystery." The slaves continued to view the loa as spirit-beings who served as intermediaries between humans and the Gran Mèt. The Catholic priests, on the other hand, taught the slaves that the Christian saints were special beings whom people could pray to, present gifts to, or do deeds in the name of. Supposedly, the saint might then help them in some way or bring them good luck. In fact, the concept of the loa and saints were so similar that the Haitians assumed they were the same spirits. Thus, it appeared, the slaves and the slave owners worshiped the same gods but called them by different names.

Voodoo worshipers easily incorporated the images of the Christian saints and other Christian symbols into their ceremonies. Even in modern Haiti, a Voodoo temple contains numerous paintings of Catholic saints as well as candles, crosses, and other objects familiar to Christian worship. One of the most popular of the saints worshiped in Voodoo is Saint Patrick. In Christian legend, he drove the snakes out of Ireland, and he is almost always pictured in the company of snakes. Voodoo believers associate Patrick with Dambala, a West African deity who takes the form of a snake. Similarly, the loa Ogou Balanjo, known as a healer, is equated with Saint Joseph, who is traditionally pictured helping small children.

The combining of African and Christian religious concepts and symbols made Voodoo a highly unusual faith. As will be seen in the next chapter, Voodoo rituals and ceremonies are both dramatic and colorful. They are also the expressions of a deep and sincere belief in powers higher than ordinary powers of human beings.

A boa constrictor coiled around the center pole of the Voodoo temple represents Dambala, the serpent god. Dambala is one of the most popular gods, or loa, in Haitian Voodoo.

Two

Voodoo Rituals

Many people in the United States and other developed countries tend to associate Voodoo only with the popular images they have seen in movies. These films usually picture Voodoo priests and worshipers as dealers in black magic and Voodoo itself as a primitive religion. Such representations are highly distorted. In fact, Voodoo, especially as it is practiced in Haiti, is a well-developed and sophisticated belief system. The tenets and practices of the Voodoo faith, like those of most other faiths, constantly address a very complex and profound issue—the ongoing relationship between human beings (including their immortal souls) and the supernatural being who controls the universe. The various rituals and ceremonies of Voodoo allow believers to explore and strengthen this mystical relationship.

The Spiritual Contract with the Loa

In Voodoo, the Gran Mèt, or Grand Master, presides over all things that exist. Followers of the Voodoo faith are highly devout and often use the phrase "if God wills" in their everyday speech. However, although they strongly revere God, believers do not usually pray directly to him. They be-

(opposite page) Voodoo practitioners toss a live chicken into the air as part of a ritual performed at an international religious congress held in 1975 in Bogota, Colombia.

Tourists watch local townsfolk perform a Voodoo ceremony in Haiti. The four women draw an elaborate design, or *vévé,* on the floor to attract the god, while a man puts rum in decorated flasks as an offering to the god.

lieve the Grand Master is so far removed from human affairs that he takes little, if any, notice of them. Thus, according to Voodoo tradition, God remains unreachable and unknowable.

Yet in Voodoo, contact with the spiritual world is both frequent and rich. To supervise the workings of nature, as well as to communicate with humans and deal with their problems, the Grand Master appointed the loa. These spirits have such qualities as intelligence, passions, hunger, strong wills, and colorful personalities. These human qualities make the loa easy for people to identify with and understand. While the Grand Master remains unreachable, the loa are willing and eager to intercede in human affairs.

The relationship between the loa and humans is based on trust and mutual give-and-take. The people are expected to conduct ceremonies honoring the loa on a regular basis. Major loa such as Ogoun and Dambala are honored in large ceremonies once or twice a year. These spirits are also honored frequently with smaller gifts of prayer and animal sacrifice. Adherents of Voodoo believe that the loa experience hunger just as humans do and that the spirits favor the blood and flesh of freshly killed animals. Thus, sacrifices of sheep, chickens, and other animals are a regular part of Voodoo worship.

According to Voodoo belief, in return for worship and sacrifice, the loa will be generous with their aid. This aid may take the form of plentiful rains and bountiful crops. Or the loa might bring improved health to the members of a family or village who suffer from illness. The spirits are also said to help people in their personal affairs. In fact, individuals have their own *mèt tet*, "master of the head," comparable to a Christian's patron saint. The mèt tet has special meaning to the person and offers him or her special protection. By offering prayer or sacrifice to the mèt tet or another loa, a person may learn from the loa how to become more generous, more devout, or more courageous. By contrast, believers hold that neglecting the worship of the loa will have negative results. These might include sickness, poor harvests, or even death.

Thus, the relationship between humanity and the loa is like a contract. Each benefits as long as the terms of the deal are faithfully executed. The terms are strong faith, prayers, and regular worship. If the terms are not met, the contract is broken, and people must be ready to suffer the consequences.

The Levels of the Soul

As in Christianity and most other faiths, the soul in Voodoo is clearly defined as being separate from the body. Followers of Voodoo say that the body contains its own special kind of energy called the *n'âme*. This is a quality of the flesh that keeps individual cells and body parts functioning. According to

As darkness falls over Rio de Janeiro, Brazil, women light candles in preparation for a sacrifice of food and liquor to Yemanja, the Mother of Waters.

believers, the n'âme is a gift from God. When a person dies, the n'âme passes into the soil and the body decays. Meanwhile, the soul has gone a different way.

The soul is divided into two parts. The first, the *gros bon ange*, or "big guardian angel," is a kind of life force shared by all people. It is what makes a person alive. This force enters the body when a person is born and leaves the body when a person dies. The gros bon ange then floats back to the Gran Mèt, where it once more becomes part of a great pool of life force. From that pool will come the gros bon anges of humans yet to be born. The second part of the soul is the *ti bon ange*, or "little guardian angel." This part consists of the individual qualities that make each person different from all others. A person's personality, will power, strength of character, and other similar qualities are all part of the the ti bon ange. Haitians use a popular comparison to explain the relationship of the two parts of the soul. The soul, they say, is like a two-tone double shadow that a person sometimes casts in the late afternoon. The dark inner shadow corresponds to the gros bon ange. The lighter outer shadow represents the ti bon ange.

The ti bon ange plays an important part in Voodoo beliefs and rituals. Supposedly, this part of the soul leaves the body at various times. During sleep, it floats away to experience dreams and returns when the person wakes up. During Voodoo ceremonies, a loa often takes temporary possession of a person. This causes the ti bon ange to float free of the body, a potentially dangerous activity. Many Voodoo adherents believe that if the ti bon ange is unprotected when it leaves a person's body, it might be captured by sorcery or damaged in some other way. In that case, the person's soul cannot pass on normally into the spirit world when the person dies. One way to prevent that is to keep on the good side of the mét tet, which can protect the soul from harm. There are no guarantees, however, that the ti bon ange will always be protected. A protecting loa may be absent when the ti bon ange is floating free of the body, at which time the soul might be damaged. Or the person may not lead a good life, causing the loa to punish the soul. The ti bon ange may then become an evil spirit, doomed to roam endlessly, bringing bad luck and misfortune to people. It is no wonder then that a great deal of Voodoo ritual revolves around the goodness, health, and protection of the soul.

Reasons for Voodoo Rituals

Followers of Voodoo practice their rituals for a number of different reasons. Some ceremonies are personal, involving the loa who guard the souls of

"Voodoo is nothing more than deplorable, idolatrous superstition."

Dean Peerman, *The Christian Century*, July 16-23, 1986

"[Voodoo] is a quintessentially democratic religion, because the believer has direct rapport with the spirit realm."

Wade Davis, *The Serpent and the Rainbow*

the members of a particular family. These rituals are practiced in response to the fortunes or misfortunes the family experiences during the course of the year. In other words, if the family is going through bad times, it is usually a sign that one or more personal spirits are displeased. In order to satisfy the offended spirit(s), the family may hold a ceremony at any time. If the family is enjoying good fortune, it may hold only a few such personal ceremonies during the course of a year. If it suffers from repeated misfortunes, the family may hold many of these ceremonies.

Occasions for Voodoo Ceremonies

Other kinds of Voodoo rituals occur at specific times during the year. These are usually large ceremonies practiced by most followers of the faith. In these ceremonies, believers honor major spirits such as Ogoun, Dambala, and Erzulie, goddess of love. Most often, such ceremonies are held on or close to the dates Catholics honor the corresponding saints. For example, two major Voodoo ceremonies take place each year in mid- to late July in northern Haiti. Thousands of Voodoo worshipers converge on the town of Saut d'Eau, also called Ville Bonheur. The town is located near a spectacular waterfall where, believers say, Our Lady of Mount Carmel, the mother of Jesus, has appeared in the palm trees near the waterfall on a number of occasions. Many associate this Catholic apparition with Ezili Freda, the Voodoo loa of love. Later in the month, in the town of Plain du Nord, worshipers gather to honor Ogoun, who is associated with the Catholic saint James the Elder.

Another important time of the year for Voodoo rituals is in late October. This is the season of the Catholic Feast of All Saints, from which Halloween developed. The spirits honored on this occasion are known as the *gede*. The gede have a number of different roles. They are spirits of death, who help guide people's souls through the spirit world. The most famous of the gede is Baron Samedi (Baron Saturday), who guards over cemeteries. The gede are also protectors of children.

The most important characteristic of the gede is their sense of humor. Believers picture them as wild-looking characters with strong personalities. The gede like to poke fun at people, society, and even themselves. For that reason, during the All Souls season, Haitians and many other Voodoo worshipers dress up as various gede in festive costumes and dance through the streets. The gede are said to be amused rather than offended by these displays. The people also dress in exaggerated costumes representing members of the community, such as doctors, farmers, mechanics, and government officials. These festivities are not a part of Voodoo ceremonies. Instead, they are part of the celebration leading up to and sometimes following the ceremonies themselves.

Several other reasons exist for Voodoo rituals. For instance, worshipers believe healing rites speed the recovery of those who are very ill. There are also various types of marriage, death, and good luck rites.

Items associated with Baron Samedi, guardian spirit of cemeteries, include a funeral director's black top hat and coat, gravediggers' tools, and a coffin with a black cross on it.

Priests and Temples

Although there are many different reasons and occasions for Voodoo ceremonies, many of the basic elements of all these ceremonies are similar. The same thing is true for most other religions. For example, Catholics hold masses for many reasons, including marriage, death, thanksgiving, and commemorating important events. Yet the basic elements involved in the mass remain the same: prayers, references to the Bible, and celebration of communion.

Among the basic elements of Voodoo ceremonies are the leaders and places of worship. A priest presides over most Voodoo ceremonies. The exception is some family ceremonies honoring personal spirits. In these cases, the head of the family leads the ritual. Voodoo priests can be male or female. The male priest is called a *houngan*, while a female priest is a *mambo*. To become either a houngan or a mambo, a person must undergo extensive training under a recognized priest for many years. Often, priests are the sons or daughters of priests who pass on their skills from one generation to another. Only when the teacher deems the student ready, and the members of the community agree, does the initiate become a practicing houngan or mambo. An elaborate feast and ceremony confirms

A worshiper prostrates herself before an altar as a sign of submission. The altar holds statues of holy beings, sacrificial food and drink, candles, and a sword in honor of Ogun, the warrior spirit.

the appointment. A given community may have one, two, or any number of priests, depending upon the needs and wishes of the people.

The temple, or holy place, where the priest performs ceremonies is called a *hounfour*. Hounfours vary according to their location. A hounfour can be a small, decrepit building in a rural area, with room enough for the priest and worshipers to congregate. It can be a larger, more elaborate building in a city. In many cases, it is a tiny room in a house or apartment used by individual families to worship personal spirits.

Hounfours have an altar, which may be quite elaborate. Many Voodoo altars are covered with candles that are burned during rituals. Christian symbols such as crucifixes and pictures of saints often clutter the altar or the walls behind it. Hounfours also have chairs, benches, or other seating for worshipers and guests.

Voodoo Ceremonies

Candles, ashes, flour, drums, dancing, praying, and reciting holy words are frequent elements in Voodoo ceremonies. So are animal sacrifices and the possession of a human body by a spirit. However, not all of these elements are a part of every ceremony. Some very simple ceremonies might only involve the lighting of candles and praying. Others consist of praying followed by the ritual killing of a goat or other animal. The longest and most involved Voodoo ceremonies usually involve most or all of the elements mentioned above. The length and complexity of a given ceremony is partly a matter of custom. Often, the more powerful and well-known spirits are honored with the most lavish ceremonies. The current relationship between spirit and worshipers is another factor. If the worshipers fear that the spirit is unusually displeased with them, they will try to appease it with a long, involved ceremony. The scene described in the prologue of this book was a part of one of these longer ceremonies.

Such a ceremony is sometimes preceded by a feast, which may take place in or near the hounfour. When it is time for the rites to begin, one or more *hounsis* appear. These are initiates, people who, for a few months, a year, or perhaps longer, help the priest conduct ceremonies. They are usually young, in their teens or early twenties. The hounsis are in the process of learning about their religion by training closely with the priests. It is usually the hounsis who undergo possession during Voodoo rituals. As the hounsis become fully initiated into temple rites, they are replaced by others eager to learn and experience. The hounsis begin the ceremony by lighting candles, a custom borrowed from Christian rituals.

A Voodoo priest traces a *vévé* using sacred cornmeal. The intricate patterns of the *vévé* are believed to attract the spirits to the ceremony. Later, the feet of entranced dancers will obliterate the *vévé*.

Next, the houngan or mambo appears. Sometimes, both may appear and conduct the ceremony together. The priest usually approaches the altar and selects a jar containing wheat or corn flour. He or she then uses the flour to trace out a *vévé*, a special design, on the floor or on the ground. The vévé are messages that help summon the spirits. Each spirit has its own vévé. The priest may then ring a bell, shake a rattle called an *asson*, or make noise in some other way to alert the spirits. As the drums begin to beat quietly in the background, the priest begins to pray. He or she appeals to Legba, the spirit of communication and the crossroad, who traditionally opens the gate to the spirit world. (Legba is often identified with Saint Peter, who is the Christian gatekeeper of heaven.) One of the chants to Legba goes:

> Father Legba, open the gate for us,
> Open the gate for us Father Legba.
> Open the gate for us father so that we
>   may enter the temple.
> On our way back, we shall thank you for
>   this favor.

Other prayers usually follow, each directed to a certain spirit or group of spirits. Depending upon the situation, the priest may chant for only a few minutes or for half an hour or more. During this time, the drums continue to beat and may become louder. The prayers are meant to honor and win the trust of the spirits. Among the most common prayers is one that recalls the earthly cycle of life and death:

> Earth, while I am yet alive,
> It is upon you that I put my trust,
> Earth who receives my body.
> We are addressing you,
> And you will understand.

After the prayers, hounsis lead the animals to be sacrificed into the hounfour. Goats, sheep, chickens, or other animals may be sacrificed, depending on which spirit or spirits are being appeased. Often, the hounsis wash the animal in preparation for the sacrifice, then feed it leaves. If the animal eats, the people believe the loa has accepted the sacrifice.

Eventually, the houngan or mambo (or both) begins to dance. At this signal, the hounsis also start dancing. The people attending the ceremony may also dance, although many may simply sway or tap their feet to the beat of the drums. Often, the drumbeats steadily grow louder and faster. Wade Davis, the American who attended the Voodoo ceremony described in the prologue of this book, tells about the unusual and powerful effect of these drums:

> Each drum had its own rhythm, its own pitch, yet there was a stunning unity to their sound that swept over the senses. The mambo's voice sliced through the night, and against the rising chords of her invocation [prayer] the drummers beat a continuous battery of sound, a resonance [vibration] so powerful and directed it had the very palm trees above swaying in sympathy.

A male Voodoo priest, or houngan, leads a group of worshipers in the invocation of a spirit, or loa, as a Voodoo ceremony begins.

A statue of St. Peter, who, in Christian lore, is heaven's gatekeeper. Voodoo adherents identify him with their gatekeeper god, Father Legba.

As the dancing continues, it becomes wilder and more energetic. Some of the dancers appear to be in a trance. It is as if their bodies are no longer under their control. Soon, one dancer, usually one of the hounsis, falls to the ground. According to Voodoo belief, he or she is now possessed by a spirit. The ti bon ange of the possessed person has floated free, and the spirit has taken control of the body. What happens next varies from ceremony to ceremony. Other dancers may immediately take the possessed person to another area of the temple. They will dress the person in the appropriate costume of the possessing spirit, then lead the person back out into the ceremony. Everyone then knows which spirit is present. In some ceremonies, this is not done. The person possessed simply begins to move and speak in ways that make it obvious to the worshipers which spirit is present.

Possession

There is no set pattern to the way a spirit acts while possessing a body, but its actions always express the personality of the loa that is possessing, or "riding," the person. The priest and hounsis treat the possessed person as though he or she *is* the spirit. They may reverently approach and offer prayers and some of the spirit's favorite foods. Or the priest may ask the spirit questions regarding some problem a person or the whole community is experiencing. The spirit may or may not answer. When the spirit does answer, it is in a voice completely different from the voice of the person being possessed. For example, if the person is a man, the spirit often speaks with a distinctly female voice. If the person is a woman, the spirit's voice may be male. This mysterious change of voice has been documented by many nonbelievers in Voodoo who have attended ceremonies.

Sometimes, the spirit does not act so calmly. As happened in the ceremony described in the prologue, the spirit may act quite violently. Leaping around the room, picking people up and tossing them, and breaking chairs and tables are frequent spirit behaviors. Grasping hot coals or other dangerous materials is also a common act. Believers accept that the spirit has the strength to lift grown people

"Both Satanism and Voodoo have potential for diabolical use."

James R. Dibble, *Mother Jones*, June 1990

"The whole idea of [Voodoo] as something dangerous and ominous is completely inaccurate. . . .[Voodoo is] a coherent world view, a system of rules, regulations, concepts, and beliefs that appear strange only to the outsider, because the outsider does not know them or appreciate them."

Wade Davis, *Saturday Review*, January/February 1986

Spirit-possessed, a Voodoo dancer swoons into the arms of a nearby worshiper. The possessed person often performs awe-inspiring feats like lifting enormous weights or handling red-hot coals without injury.

off the ground as if they were rag dolls. And believers are not surprised when the possessed body is not injured by the hot coals and other dangerous materials. According to the faith, spirits cannot be harmed by such things. Yet outside observers find these occurrences very strange and difficult to explain.

At the height of the ceremony, the priest or the hounsis sacrifice the animals. Most often, they slit the throats and allow some of the blood to drain into a special bowl. The possessed hounsis may drink some of the blood. Although the spirit does not actually eat the body of the animal during the ceremony, the worshipers believe the offering has appeased the spirit's hunger. To honor the spirit and complete the sacrifice, the worshipers may later

Animal sacrifice is sometimes part of the Voodoo ceremony. The worshipers believe that the offering of an animal pleases the spirit.

cook and eat the animal. This, they believe, further satisfies the spirit's hunger as well as brings the participants in the ceremony good fortune.

Exhausting Rituals

The same sequence of events that occurred during the earlier dancing may now be repeated. One or more other worshipers may undergo possession. The drumming, dancing, and other activities sometimes continue well into the night. If a drummer faints from exhaustion, another drummer immediately takes his or her place.

Eventually, the spirits depart, and the worshipers, even those who did not undergo possession, are exhausted. They go home to sleep before they must get up and begin their day's work. Although they are tired from the night of worship, they are also satisfied and secure in the feeling that they have been in touch with the spirit world. They have fulfilled their part of the contract with the spirits. They go about their business believing that the spirits, also satisfied, will now watch over them favorably. There may not be another such elaborate ceremony in the community for a week, a month, or many months. But there will be many smaller rituals and gift offerings to the spirits. Some believers worship several times a week or even every day. Most followers of Voodoo are extremely devout. For them, religion is not a casual act to be practiced now and then or only in times of trouble. Their faith is an integral part of the fabric of their everyday lives. It is with them always.

Three

Zombies and Magic

The primary focus of Voodoo is the positive, healthy relationship between humans and spirits. Most often, Voodoo is associated with ordinary religious worship. There is, however, a darker side to Voodoo, a side associated with evil. Believers refer to the darker side of the faith as the "work of the left hand," or "left-handed Voodoo."

A False Stereotype

Many outsiders mistakenly think left-handed Voodoo is typical of Voodoo in general. Left-handed Voodoo has to do with sorcery, or black magic, the summoning of evil spirits, and zombies, the soulless bodies of people who have been raised from the dead. Zombies were not part of the African religions from which Voodoo evolved. Belief in such beings developed in Haiti and is unique to Haitian Voodoo. The belief in werewolves, creatures that are half human and half wolf, is also a part of left-handed Voodoo.

These supernatural elements have become part of the false stereotype of Voodoo accepted by most people outside of Haiti and the Caribbean. This stereotype developed partly because of books written by European and American authors in the late

(opposite page) A reanimated corpse, or zombie, rises from its grave to do the bidding of its Voodoo master. Modern movies have focused on zombies and other aspects of the less common, dark side of Voodoo instead of the much more prevalent positive side. Hence, most people outside of Haiti have misconceptions about Voodoo.

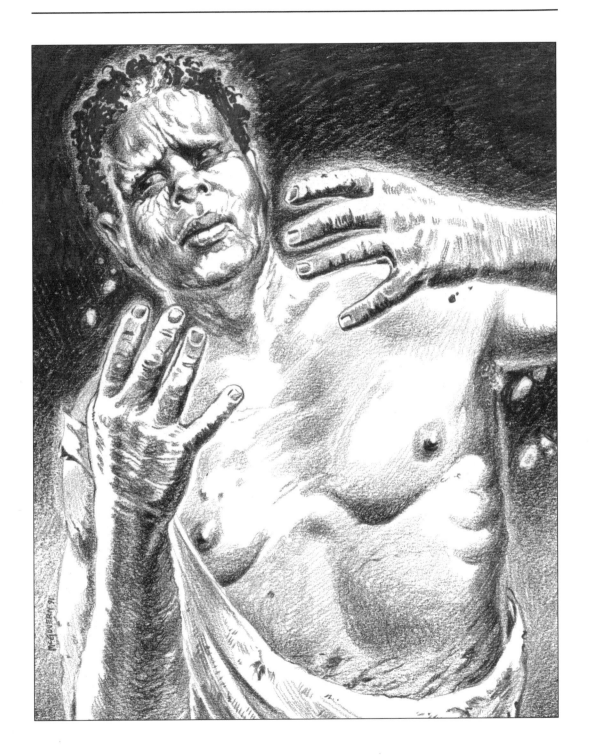

"You hear stories all the time, but you can never actually find a zombie."

Leslie Desmangles, Haitian religion scholar

"I am absolutely convinced that zombies exist. I have seen them for myself."

Lemarque Douyon, chief of psychiatry for the government of Haiti

1800s and early 1900s. These books made exaggerated, sensational, and even false claims about Voodoo. Some of the writers never traveled to Haiti and simply repeated unreliable rumors and other hearsay. The writers who did go to Haiti were disappointed with what they found there. They had expected to find shocking, primitive rites filled with black magic, human sacrifice, and other sinister elements. Instead, they found a legitimate religion that reflected the positive aspects of Haitian life. But for European and American readers at the time, this was too tame. They wanted to be shocked and horrified. In order to sell books, many authors distorted the facts of left-handed Voodoo or completely fabricated their own facts.

One of the most notable distortions of Voodoo was Spencer St. John's book *Haiti, or The Black Republic*, published in 1884. St. John accumulated all the weird and exotic tales he had heard about Voodoo worship in Haiti. One of his most sensational claims was that Voodoo priests sometimes practiced human sacrifice and cannibalism. Spencer said that a Voodoo priest had confessed to cooking and eating a young girl during a ceremony. Spencer either did not know or chose not to reveal that the priest had confessed to this false accusation under torture. Haitian government officials wanted an excuse to imprison him.

Voodoo on the Big Screen

Later, the left-handed Voodoo stereotype was popularized in films. Beginning in the 1930s, for instance, Hollywood movies often portrayed the people of Haiti and other Caribbean islands worshiping evil spirits and becoming zombies. *The Walking Dead* (1936), *I Walked with a Zombie* (1943), and *Voodoo Man* (1949) perpetuated the stereotype. These and other films unflatteringly characterize the black inhabitants of the Caribbean. They are shown as ignorant, backward people obsessed with

A New Orleans Voodoo practitioner called "The Chicken Man" shows two Voodoo dolls he used to try to influence the 1988 national elections. The doll on the left bears the name "Duke" for Democratic presidential candidate Michael Dukakis. The doll on the right represents the Democrats in general. Dolls are not generally used in Voodoo practices outside of New Orleans.

werewolves, casting spells and curses, and creating zombies to terrorize their enemies. The films frequently show people sticking pins in or burning Voodoo dolls. These dolls are supposed to represent people, who feel pain or die when the dolls are mutilated. These early films inspired later movies that also falsely depict Voodoo. One example is *The Believers* (1987). It shows Voodoo priests in the United States using their magic powers to kill innocent people in brutal fashion. None of these films depict Voodoo as a legitimate religion, and all of them completely distort left-handed Voodoo.

In reality, the practice of left-handed Voodoo is

rare. And when people do use it, it only occasionally involves the elements of the popular stereotype. Human sacrifice and cannibalism have never played a part in left-handed Voodoo. Also, the use of Voodoo dolls is almost unheard of in most places people practice Voodoo. No one uses such dolls in Haiti. The only recorded serious use of them was among American Voodoo worshipers in the New Orleans area in the 1800s and early 1900s. Followers of Voodoo do not take very seriously other components of left-handed Voodoo portrayed in the stereotypes either. For example, although many people in Haiti and other islands used to believe in werewolves, few do today. Like witches or bogeymen in the United States and other countries, werewolves in Haiti are legendary rather than real beings. Werewolves are part of the island folk heritage, surviving as children's stories and tall tales told to impress visitors and tourists. The few people in Haiti who really do believe in werewolves are no different than the few gullible people in every other country who believe in such things.

Evil Spirits

On the other hand, most followers of Voodoo do believe in the existence of evil spirits. Just as many Christians accept the existence of demons and fallen angels, believers in Voodoo hold that some inhabitants of the spirit world are bad. Believers recognize that spirits, like people, have the potential for either good or bad deeds. No one knows for sure what makes a person or spirit become evil. But, according to believers, evil is an accepted part of both the present life and the afterlife. In fact, like the two sides of a coin, the good and evil cannot be separated. As one Haitian told Wade Davis, "Haiti will teach you that good and evil are one. We never confuse them, nor do we keep them apart."

In the Voodoo faith, most spirits are good and beneficial. Only a few are evil, and these seldom harm people who are on good terms with the good spirits. Through the use of sorcery, however, evil spirits may be summoned and enticed to perform mischief. For instance, Baka is an evil spirit who, when on earth, takes the form of an animal. Supposedly, contact with Baka can bring bad luck or various misfortunes.

Bokors

Houngans who specialize in sorcery are called *bokors*. Such "dark" priests practice sorcery either to earn money or for their own personal reasons. Since they ply their trade for money, most Haitians think of them as shady professional people. A few priests alternate between the duties of houngan and bokor. Believers tend to accept the existence of bokors as a matter of course. Yet the magical work

Werewolves, creatures part human and part wolf, are part of the folklore of Haiti. Most modern Haitians do not believe werewolves really exist—but they may enjoy frightening gullible tourists with werewolf stories.

of the bokor lies outside the regular framework of the Voodoo religion. It is never a part of the usual religious ceremonies.

Followers of Voodoo do not necessarily think all of the bokor's magic is evil. Instead, they often look upon it as a kind of disreputable shortcut. For example, one of the most common feats supposedly performed by bokors is changing the weather. The bokor might convince an evil spirit to make it rain. In this case, the result is beneficial to everyone. What most people object to is the method. It is far more accepted to pray and sacrifice to beneficent spirits. Paying a bokor money, no matter what the goal, is usually frowned upon, and few people actually engage bokors.

Bokors use various powders, herbs, poisons, and chants to create their magic. They place the powders and herbs on the ground in certain patterns while chanting, similar to the way a houngan or mambo makes a veve in regular Voodoo. In this way, the bokor may summon an evil spirit. Sacrifices are also involved, since, believers hold, evil spirits are as hungry as any others. The bokor asks the spirit to grant a favor, and the spirit either agrees or declines.

The Zombie Astral

Bokors also claim to be able to capture a person's ti bon ange, the part of the soul that carries the personality and memory. Many believers refer to this captured spirit as the *zombie astral*. According to tradition, the person who pays the bokor to capture the soul then can control the will of the person from which the soul has been taken. When Wade Davis visited Haiti in the early 1980s, he watched a bokor at work. Using his magic, the bokor attempted to capture someone's ti bon ange. Later, a Haitian government official told Davis, "In that bottle was the soul of a human being, the control of which is an ominous power. It is a ghost, or like a dream; it wanders at the command of the one who possesses it. It is a zombie astral captured from the victim by the magic of the bokor."

Out of the Grave

Perhaps the most famous and most misunderstood aspect of left-handed Voodoo is the *zombie cadavre*, or walking zombie. According to Haitian legend, as well as Hollywood films, zombies are the bodies of people who have died, been buried, and later resurrected. The bokor accomplishes this process, called zombification, through black magic. He or she uses strange and potent powders and poisons, usually placed on the doorstep of the intended victim. When the victim steps on these powders, the magic enters the body through the soles of the feet. Soon the victim dies and has a funeral. Within three days, the bokor sneaks into the cemetery, recites a magical chant, then calls the victim's name several times. The victim awakens as a zombie, which the bokor digs up. Another version of the legend claims that the zombie digs its own way out of the grave.

The zombie must do the bidding of the person who paid the bokor. The person may have wanted the victim made a zombie in order to get revenge. Or the person may want the zombie to perform slave labor. Usually, zombies are depicted as having no soul, no memory of their former lives, and no ability to talk or reason. Supposedly, they are condemned to wander the countryside, usually at night, or work mindlessly as slaves in the fields. In some parts of Haiti, legends say there is one way to partially revive a zombie: If someone puts salt on the zombie's tongue, it will regain some of its memory and be able to talk. But, believers warn, this is dangerous. The zombie might seek revenge on those who caused its death and others.

Most Haitians admit they have never seen a zombie, but they are convinced such beings exist. Haitians find the idea of becoming a zombie both

"The *zombi* is a beast of burden which his master exploits without mercy, making him work in the fields, weighing him down with labor."

Alfred Métraux, *Voodoo in Haiti*

"Given the availability of cheap labor and the physical condition of the zombies, there is no economic incentive to create a force of indentured labor."

Wade Davis, *American Scientist*, July/August 1987

repulsive and frightening. Therefore, in Haiti, by tradition, zombies are complete outcasts, feared or shunned by every member of society. This has led some Haitians to treat the corpses of their dead in unusual ways. As American researcher Nathan Kline put it:

> Haitians believe that their sorcerers have the power to raise innocent individuals from their graves and sell them as slaves. It is to prevent such a fate that family members may kill the body of the dead a second time, sometimes plunging a knife into the heart of the cadaver, sometimes severing the head in the coffin.

With the body disfigured in this way, Haitians believe, the bokor is unable to complete the process of zombification. The dead person may now rest in peace. However, many Haitians cannot bring themselves to mutilate the bodies of their loved ones. According to believers, this leaves the cemeteries filled with corpses with the potential of becoming zombies.

Return to the Living

Although most Haitians insist that zombies exist, over the years there have been few documented cases of zombies. A documented case is one in which all the facts and claims have been verified by respected authorities. Perhaps the best-known documented case of zombification involved a Haitian farmer named Clairvius Narcisse. On April 30, 1962, Narcisse entered a Haitian hospital complaining of fever, body aches, and a general feeling of weakness. As doctors examined him, he began spitting up blood. His condition got steadily worse, and about two days later, the doctors pronounced him dead. Narcisse's sister Angelina arrived at the hospital and witnessed that the body was indeed that of her brother. A day later, on May 3, the Narcisse family buried him in the cemetery near his native town of l'Estere.

Eighteen years later, in 1980, Angelina was shopping in the l'Estere marketplace. Suddenly, she says, her brother Narcisse approached her. Naturally, she was startled and afraid. But she soon regained her composure and begged to know what had happened. According to Narcisse, he had been zombified by a bokor. After being buried, the bokor had dug him up, beaten him, and taken him to a farm on the other side of Haiti. There, he worked as a field slave with several other zombies.

One day, Narcisse claimed, one of the zombies killed the slave master and the zombies all escaped. In time, he regained most of his memory. Although his speech remained slurred and his muscles weak, he was no longer a zombie, a fact he was at a loss to explain. This comforted him, but he was afraid to return home. He suspected that his brother had hired the bokor to make him a zombie, and he

The heavy above-ground tombstones in this typical Haitian cemetery were designed to prevent bokors from making zombies of the dead.

feared facing his brother again.

So, Narcisse had wandered around Haiti for the next sixteen years, working as a migrant farm laborer. Eventually, he heard that his brother had died, and he mustered the courage to return home.

Narcisse soon became well known in Haiti. Not only were there few proven cases of zombification, there were even fewer known cases of zombies returning to the world of the living. Therefore, Narcisse was an oddity. He told his story to the newspapers, and government officials questioned him. In 1981, British TV reporters interviewed him and made a documentary film about his experiences. One investigator wanted to test Narcisse to see if he was an imposter. There was a chance that the real Narcisse had actually died, and the imposter was pretending to be Narcisse in order to inherit his land. The investigator asked Narcisse many questions about Narcisse's childhood that only the real Narcisse and his closest family members could know. Narcisse answered all the questions correctly. In addition, more than two hundred residents of l'Estere testified that he was the real Narcisse.

Other Known Zombies

Narcisse's case was not the only one involving modern-day Haitian zombies. Because of the publicity surrounding the case, other people came forward with similar stories. Some of these people had returned to society before Narcisse but had received little publicity. One of these cases involved a middle-aged woman named Nategette Joseph. According to her friends and relatives, she had died in 1966 after being injured during a dispute over land. In 1980, coincidentally the same year that Narcisse resurfaced, people in her village saw her walking around the streets. Fearing she was a zombie, most of the villagers refused to go near her. Finally, a local police officer approached her. He had known her well and had pronounced her dead years before.

He positively identified her as the same Nategette Joseph. Like Narcisse, she could talk and walk, although with some difficulty. Seeing that she was no longer a zombie, some members of her family took her in.

In 1976, thirty-year-old Francina Illeus entered a local hospital in Haiti. She was suffering from severe digestive problems, as well as dizziness and weakness. Doctors treated then released her. A few days later, she died in her home, and a local town official pronounced her dead. She was buried in the town cemetery, where dozens of people saw her body in the coffin and witnessed it being lowered into the ground. Yet three years later, some farmers saw her sitting in a public market. They summoned Illeus's mother. Although Illeus was pale, thin from

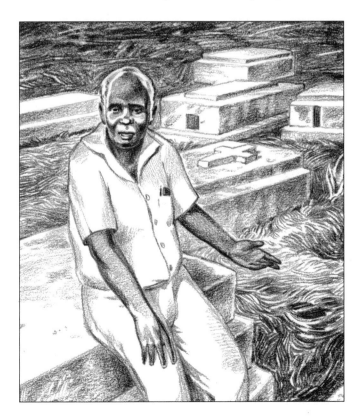

This drawing depicts Haitian Clairvius Narcisse pointing to the grave where he had been buried after his death in 1962. Narcisse claims a *bokor*, or Voodoo sorcerer, made him a zombie and used him for slave labor until he escaped. Narcisse cannot explain why he is no longer a zombie.

lack of food, and unable to speak, her mother immediately recognized her. The mother verified that it was her daughter by a childhood scar on Illeus's forehead. Immediately, her family and friends rushed to her grave and dug it up. They found her coffin filled with rocks. Afterward, a Haitian doctor cared for Illeus, trying to help her readjust to society. But her eyes remained blank, and she found it difficult to walk. Eventually, she began talking again, but only in a high, thin voice. She showed few emotions and had few memories of the past.

Questions Never Before Asked

Many Haitians point to the cases of Clairvius Narcisse and the others as proof that people have been buried and later walked among the living. The stories do not explain *how* the people became zombies, but for followers of Voodoo, such explanations are unnecessary. They accept as a matter of faith that a bokor's magic can cause zombification. For them, Narcisse's story is supported by their religious beliefs.

The British and other foreigners who examined Narcisse's case were perplexed, however. They had been brought up in societies that taught that magic is not real. Thanks to the popular stereotype, they had simply dismissed the idea of zombies and Voodoo in general as primitive and silly. Yet after examining Narcisse's story, they could not deny that he had been buried and then somehow resurrected. This raised many questions about zombies that foreigners had never seriously asked before. How does one become a zombie? Can the dead actually be brought back to life? Also, *why* does someone become a zombie? Do the bokor and slave masters select victims at random, or do they single out specific people for specific reasons? The role of the slave masters raised still another question. Because their ancestors were slaves, modern Haitians hate the concept of slavery. How could slave masters exist in such a society?

The publicity about Narcisse reached the United States and other countries, and many other foreigners began asking the same questions. Researchers traveled to Haiti in the 1980s to investigate the zombie phenomenon. They studied Voodoo and attended Voodoo ceremonies. They traveled with bokors and bargained for their secrets. A few researchers managed to attend special secret ceremonies that no foreigners knew existed. As will be seen in the next chapter, these investigations finally lifted the veil of mystery that had surrounded zombies. Zombies, the researchers discovered, were very real, although not in the way the legends described. But the studies also had some unexpected results. In their efforts to eliminate the mystery of the zombies, the researchers came face-to-face with some of the basic mysteries of Voodoo. These, they found, were not so easy to explain in a logical, rational manner.

Four

Scientists Examine Voodoo

The stories of Clairvius Narcisse and other zombies, though well documented, seem strange and mysterious to most people living outside of Haiti. Most Americans, for example, find the idea of making dead people come back to life illogical and unbelievable. Generally, they accept the testimony of doctors and scientists who state that once a person is dead, the blood ceases to circulate, and the brain cells die. After a few minutes at most, the person cannot be revived. This is one reason many Americans and others foreign to Haiti quickly dismissed Narcisse's story.

Another reason for being skeptical about zombies was lack of hard evidence. Although his friends and relatives testified that he was the real Narcisse, skeptics say, they might have been mistaken. Eighteen years had elapsed since his confirmed death. People's memories can fade over the course of time. Also, there was plenty of time for an imposter who looked like Narcisse to learn all about his childhood and later life. To most foreigners, anything having to do with zombies, or Voodoo itself for that matter, was pure nonsense. Writer Barbara Christensen summed up this view in her book, *The Magic and Meaning of Voodoo.*

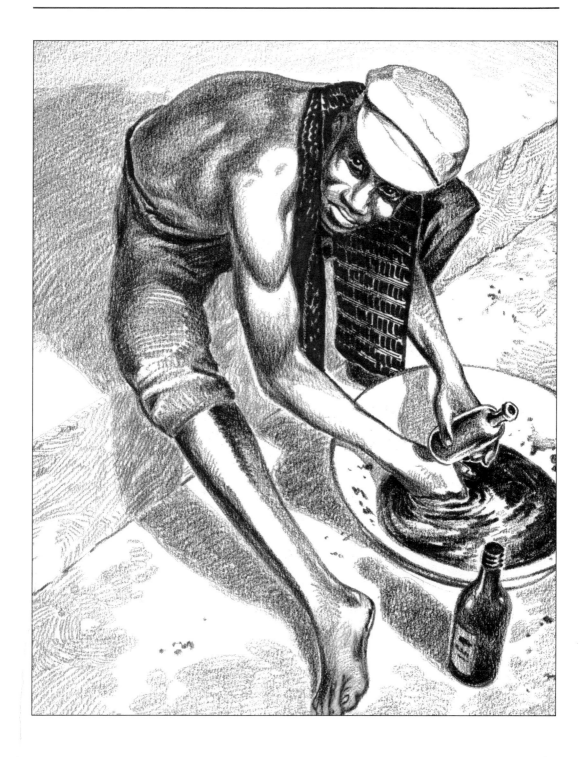

"[The case of Clairvius Narcisse] shows that one of the most exploited of folk beliefs has a logical basis."

Wade Davis, *The Serpent and the Rainbow*

"I actually feel [Davis's theory] is an issue of fraud in science."

Pharmacologist C.Y. Kao, State University of New York Downstate Medical Center in Brooklyn

"Voodoo," she said, "is only a collection of superstitious beliefs."

Despite those who dismissed the accounts of Narcisse's case, a few scientists were fascinated by his story and other stories involving zombies. These researchers did not believe people could be brought back to life once they were dead but that did not mean the zombie phenomenon was not real. Perhaps, the scientists suggested, there was a logical explanation for zombies. If so, it would have to account for all the claims made by Narcisse and other former zombies. Such a scientific theory would also have to explain the claims made about zombification by bokors and followers of Voodoo in general.

A Powerful Drug

In 1981, Heinz Lehman, a professor of psychiatry at McGill University in Montreal, Canada, and New York psychiatrist Dr. Nathan Kline discussed the Narcisse case. They also examined many other cases of supposed zombies as well as stories of how bokors claimed to create zombies. Lehman and Kline were intrigued by zombie powders and poisons and suggested a theory to explain zombification. They agreed that there was a possibility the "magical" powders might contain a powerful drug. The drug might somehow slow down the victim's body functions so much that he or she would appear dead. Friends and relatives would bury the victim, and later, the bokor who concocted the drug might dig up the victim and administer an antidote. According to this theory, the victim never really dies. The bokor or person who hired him continues to feed the victim powerful drugs that keep him or her disoriented and helpless. The victim remains a zombie for as long as its master administers the drug.

Lehman and Kline realized their theory could not be true unless drugs like the ones their theory depended on actually exist. In fact, this was what had drawn them to the zombie phenomenon in the first place. They wanted to find new drugs that could be used as anesthetics in surgery. The anesthetics now used to render patients unconscious usually work well, but sometimes anesthetics kill patients. Said Kline, "If we could find a new drug which made the patient utterly insensible to pain, and paralyzed, and another which harmlessly returned him to normal consciousness, it could revolutionize modern surgery."

According to Kline, such drugs would have other beneficial uses. "Anesthesia is only the beginning," he said. "NASA once asked me to consider the possible application of psychoactive [mind-altering] drugs in the space program. . . . They . . . were concerned with how they were going to keep the restless astronauts occupied during extended interplanetary missions. The zombie poison could provide a fascinating model for experiments in artificial hibernation."

The Search for the Zombie Poison

Lehman and Kline were convinced that the zombie poison was real because drugs with some of the zombifying properties were already known. They were familiar with the work of several experts on plant drugs, including famed Harvard anthropologist and botanist Richard Evans Schultes. In the 1940s, Schultes had investigated thousands of plants in the Amazon rain forest of South America. The local natives used some of these plants for medicinal purposes. During his research, Schultes discovered curare, a powerful plant poison that the natives used on the tips of their arrows and darts. When they fired an arrow at a monkey, the animal lost all muscular control, collapsed, and became completely helpless. Usually, the poison did not kill. Schultes brought curare back to the United States, and chemists analyzed it. From the drug, they developed D-tubocurarine, a powerful muscle relaxant. It is used extensively in modern surgery.

South American Indians hunt small game with a blowgun that shoots poison darts. The poison is made from plants and animals similar to those used by Haitian bokors to make zombie poison.

The zombie poison, Lehman and Kline reasoned, might be similar to curare.

In 1982, Lehman and Kline discussed their theory with ethnobotanist Wade Davis, who was then completing his degree at Harvard University. Davis's specialty was studying the place of plants in human cultures. Lehman and Kline asked Davis to travel to Haiti to search for the zombie poison, and Davis agreed to go. Reaching Haiti, he quickly realized that finding such a substance and obtaining a sample to take home would not be easy. Most native Haitians did not want to talk about zombies or any other aspects of left-handed Voodoo. Such knowledge was cloaked in secrecy. To get what he needed, Davis would have to gain the people's trust. Also, it was important to learn how the zombie poison, if it existed, fit into the larger framework of Voodoo itself. So, Davis attended several Voodoo ceremonies. He also became friendly with local officials who introduced him to houngans, hounsis, and other people involved in the religion. In addition, he interviewed some supposed former zombies, including Clairvius Narcisse.

Eventually, Davis met a bokor and hired him to create some of the poison. Davis pretended that he wanted to eliminate a personal enemy and insisted that the powder should be as powerful as possible. Later, Davis had the powder analyzed and found it to be more or less harmless. The bokor, unwilling to reveal his secrets, had purposely cheated him.

Davis then went to a houngan who said he knew about the zombie poison. The houngan insisted that zombies are uninteresting and a waste of time. They are not nearly as profound and unexplainable, he said, as the mysteries of the Voodoo religion itself. Davis found this significant. The houngan was strongly suggesting that zombification is not as magical a procedure as the legends report. The more Davis learned from the houngan, the more he became convinced that making a zombie was an explainable process. This gave strong support to Lehman and Kline's theory. Davis continued to press the houngan for a sample of the powder used to create zombies.

Deadly Toads and Fish

Finally, the houngan, claiming that he had consulted some secret contacts, provided Davis with some zombie poison. It contained a number of very toxic ingredients, including some poisonous plants. The powder also contained parts from some extremely poisonous animals. There were at least two kinds of poisonous toads and a puffer fish, which secretes tetrodotoxin, a deadly poison. The poison is obtained by drying and then grinding up the puffer fish.

According to the houngan, a single zombie poison does not exist. There are a number of different mixtures, each of which has a slightly different physical effect. For example, one produces simu-

"The poison causes a profound paralysis, suppressing the metabolic rate to the point where the victim may live for hours or even days on the amount of oxygen trapped in the coffin."

Susan Katz, *Newsweek,* February 24, 1986

"The trauma of being buried alive and the knowledge that one is a social outcast is perhaps as potent as any drug."

Sharon Begley, *Newsweek,* February 22, 1988

This puffer fish inflates itself with seawater as a defense against attack. The puffers are also a primary source of one of the deadliest nerve poisons on earth, tetrodotoxin. Voodoo bokors often use puffer fish in zombie poisons.

lated death almost immediately after reaching the bloodstream. Another version makes a victim feel ill and waste away slowly over the course of many days. Some versions, said the houngan, the bokor puts in the victim's food. Others the victim absorbs through the skin. Davis remembered that the zombie legends spoke of powders placed on people's doorsteps and absorbed through the soles of the feet.

The houngan also told Davis about the antidote to the zombie poison. This, said the houngan, the bokor feeds to the victim after removing him or her from the grave. The antidote contains ingredients such as sweet potato, cane syrup, and a powerful drug. The drug comes from the tropical plant *Datura stramonium*, popularly known in the Caribbean as the "zombie's cucumber." This antidote, claimed the houngan, does more than just help revive the victim. The victim later receives more doses of the concoction, which keeps him or her in a drugged state. In this state, the zombie cannot function as a normal person, and its master can easily control it.

Evaluating the Zombie Powders

Davis's findings were very controversial. Some scientists claimed that tetrodotoxin could not be part of the zombie powder. This poison is so lethal, they said, that it would kill the victims outright. There would be no way of reviving them later. According to Davis, the lethal effects of tetrodotoxin are slightly reduced when the substance is mixed with certain plants and other ingredients. Davis claimed that, like curare, the right mixture of tetrodotoxin could produce an anesthetic effect. This effect, said Davis, is somewhat like a coma. The victim shows little or no pulse, lowered breathing, and lowered body temperature. Under the right circumstances, the victim would appear to be dead.

The antidote to the zombie poison is made from the tropical plant *Datura stramonium*.

Davis encountered other critics who claimed that he had not collected enough samples of the poison. One or two samples, they said, are not enough with which to study a phenomenon so widespread. Perhaps, they suggested, Davis's sample was badly or fraudulently prepared. To be sure it was genuine, he would have to collect dozens of samples from all over Haiti. Some scientists claimed that the poison Davis had collected, when tested, produced no anesthetic effect. To them, this seemed to suggest that Davis had purposely brought back a phony sample. Dr. C.Y. Kao of the State University of New York said that Davis's work appeared fraudulent. Dr. Bo Holmstedt, of the Karolinska Institute in Stockholm, Sweden, did not think Davis was a fraud, but he suggested that Davis might have ignored certain facts he uncovered in Haiti, facts that would weaken the Lehman-Kline theory. This made Davis's work unscientific, he said.

Davis responded that he had not ignored or overlooked any important facts during his stay in Haiti. He had, he said, tried diligently to uncover the truth. He insisted that he was not afraid to admit the existence of information that seemed to refute the theory he had been sent to prove. When the first sample from the bokor had turned out to be phony, for example, he had been the first to recognize it. Davis agreed that having more samples to examine would be better from a scientific standpoint. But it had taken him many months just to get one houngan to trust him enough to reveal the secret. Obtaining dozens of samples from highly secretive houngans and bokors all over the island would be nearly impossible. Davis also denied that the second sample was fraudulent. Said Davis, chemists at Columbia University and the University of Lausanne in France had verified that it contained tetrodotoxin and the other ingredients he had described.

The Social Aspect of Zombies

Davis stuck by his research. "I had arrived in Haiti," he said, "to investigate zombies. A poison had been found and identified, [and] a substance had been indicated that was chemically capable of maintaining a person so poisoned in a zombie state." But Davis insisted that the poison and antidote themselves constituted the least important evidence about zombies that he discovered in Haiti. According to Davis, many local Haitians confirmed the Lehman-Kline theory simply by confiding to him how and why zombies were created.

Regarding *how* zombies are created, said Davis, there is no doubt that it is a physical process involving chemicals and drugs. The local houngans, bokors, and other experts Davis talked to admitted

"It is clear that the creation of zombies entails an extremely sophisticated melding of the sciences of pharmacology and psychology."

Nick Jordan, *Psychology Today*, May 1984

"We still don't have all the answers, but we're trying to unravel this mystery [zombies]."

Lemarque Douyon, chief of psychiatry for the government of Haiti

that bokors give their victims powders that simulate death. These locals know full well that victims of zombification never actually die. In fact, bokors are extremely careful not to mix the ingredients of the powder incorrectly for fear of permanently killing the victim. A bokor admitted to Davis that if a person is "too" dead, he or she cannot be resurrected as a zombie. In fact, Davis discovered, there are often cases where the victims do die and never make it

Harvard botanist Wade Davis went to Haiti to find out how zombies are made. He returned home with malaria, the various Voodoo items pictured here, and the secret of the zombie makers.

out of the grave to receive the antidote. Thus, the zombies of legend, dead people brought back to life, do not exist. And the people most responsible for creating zombies are well aware of this fact.

Yet, as Davis and other researchers who have visited Haiti have confirmed, beings called zombies do exist, even if these beings never actually died. They are people who have been poisoned and drugged. They are people without memories and with little or no will to resist the control of others. Someone purposely selected them to become zombies. The most important question surrounding zombies, then, is: *Why* do bokors and others single out a person to become a zombie?

This, as it turned out, was the most important contribution made by Davis and other modern researchers to knowledge about the zombie phenomenon. Through their persistence in gaining the trust of local Haitians, they finally unlocked the mystery of why zombies are created. Davis and the others found that zombification is part of the complex social structure of Haiti, a structure in which special secret societies exist.

Secret Societies

The existence of secret societies in Haiti had been pointed out by other foreigners who had earlier visited the island. In the 1930s and 1940s, for instance, Zora Neale Hurston, a young American woman studying anthropology, journeyed to Haiti. She discovered that Haiti had several secret societies that met at night in remote places. Supposedly, ordinary citizens of Haiti knew that these societies existed, but they almost never talked about them. They feared going out at night, believing members of the societies could change themselves into large cats, wolves, and other animals. These animals roamed the countryside attacking travelers and doing other evil deeds. Hurston never broke through the veil of secrecy to attend a meeting of one of the societies. All her information came from interviews with the few people who would talk to her about the organizations. Because she could not offer any first-hand evidence about the societies, most American anthropologists doubted their existence.

Although Hurston described the secret societies, she never associated them specifically with zombi-fication. It was Wade Davis and other researchers of the 1970s and 1980s who established this connection. They too heard the stories about people being afraid of evil animals roaming the night. But, they found, few Haitians actually believe such tales. The average Haitian is apparently more afraid of other powers the societies hold. The power most feared is that of turning someone into a zombie. That power, the researchers found, along with the secret societies themselves, evolved out of the events of Haiti's unique history. This explains why zombies are mainly a Haitian phenomenon. Thus, Davis and the others realized, to understand zombies fully, one had to understand how the Haitian secret societies came to be.

The Terror of the Maroons

Haiti's secret societies originated during the island's colonial days as Saint Domingue, when the French used masses of slaves to operate huge sugar and coffee plantations. As mentioned earlier, the French caught and punished many slaves who ran away. But some runaways managed to elude the French soldiers and dogs who chased them. The French called these successful runaways Maroons. The Maroons fled deep into remote jungle areas, built forts, tended their own fields, and became self-sufficient. But they wanted more than freedom. Says Wade Davis, "These were Africans who would take responsibility for their fate, men who sought not just to survive but to fight and to seek revenge for the weight of injustice that had tormented their people." The Maroons became guerrilla fighters, who periodically attacked the French plantations and tried to free other slaves.

No one knows for sure how many Maroons there were at any given time. But some historians estimate that in the late 1700s there may have been over forty thousand. The French often sent expeditions of soldiers into the hills to capture the Maroons. Few of these expeditions met with success, and some simply disappeared without a trace. By 1770, there were so many bands of Maroons terrorizing the countryside that most of the French were afraid to go out at night or wander beyond the safety of towns.

To protect themselves, the Maroons strictly con-

An engraving depicts eighteenth-century runaway Haitian slaves, or Maroons, battling French soldiers sent to recapture them. The Maroons began the secret societies that still exist in Haiti today. They also passed down the West Africans' knowledge of natural drugs and poisons.

trolled their own societies and were very careful about admitting new members. There was always the chance that a runaway slave was a spy for the French. The Maroons held elaborate initiations, most of which involved severe, self-inflicted pain. They had secret passwords and handshakes and swore allegiance to their communities. The members of these communities, many of whom had been born in Africa, practiced African religions. They also passed on traditional African knowledge about plant and animal poisons and drugs. Evidence shows they were already using these poisons and drugs in the 1700s to punish spies and traitors. Sometimes the Maroons poisoned and killed wrongdoers. At other times, they forced them to work as slaves in the Maroon camps. The Maroon houngans soon learned that these slaves were easier to control when drugged. These poisons and drugs were the precursors of the zombie powders.

Poisoning the French

The poisons the Maroons concocted were so effective that one Maroon leader, Macandal, planned to use them against the French. His goal was to slowly poison the French planters and soldiers until they were all dead or until the survivors fled Saint Domingue. Maroons secretly handed out doses of poison to slaves working for whites. As Davis puts it:

> To their horror, the whites found themselves in a trap of their own making, dependent on the very people who were the agents of their doom. The poison appeared everywhere: baked into bread, in medicine vials, in kegs of ale lifted directly from the ships and drunk because the water from the wells could no longer be trusted. . . . The terror of the whites gave way to rage, and innocent slaves were flayed alive. The slightest suspicion of collaboration with the poisoners meant a horrible death.

In all, more than six thousand French died of poison during Macandal's rebellion. Finally, under

"Is it really the case that healthy people have died in a day, or three days, because they know they were victims of sorcery? Who has seen this happen with his own eyes?"

G. Lewis, medical anthropologist

"As in all belief, the power of suggestion is the most potent ingredient. . . . As in all magic, it is the magical powers of the mind which accomplish true sorcery."

Charles M. Gandolfo, proprietor of the Voodoo Museum in New Orleans threat of being burned alive, some of Macandal's followers betrayed him. When the French tried to burn him at the stake, he broke free. The French guards claimed they grabbed him and threw him into the fire. Macandal's followers, however, insisted that he escaped. History remains unclear.

Birth of the Secret Societies

The Maroons led other slave revolts in Saint Domingue. Eventually, in 1791, a grand revolt began that finally succeeded. Maroon agents sneaked onto plantations all over the island and led secret meetings, each attended by hundreds of slaves. They held Voodoo ceremonies and plotted the downfall of the French. Maroon leader Boukman Dutty became the head of the rebellion. At a meeting in August 1791, he declared:

> God who made the sun that shines on us from above . . . is looking down upon us. He sees what the whites are doing. The God of the whites asks for crime; ours [the loa] desire only blessings. But this God [Ogoun] who is good directs you to vengeance! . . . Cast aside the image of the God of the whites who thirsts for our tears and pay heed to the voice of liberty speaking to our hearts.

The revolt began on August 21 and quickly engulfed the whole island.

After several years of fighting, some black leaders, the most notable being Toussaint L'Ouverture, switched their allegiance back to the French. L'Ouverture turned on Dutty and other Maroon leaders, destroying several Maroon strongholds. L'Ouverture did this because the French promised they would abolish slavery and allow blacks to rule the colony. In return, Saint Domingue would remain a French colony and continue to supply France with sugar and other crops. The French later betrayed L'Ouverture and sent troops to crush the rebellion. The French failed, and Saint Domingue became free of foreign domination in 1803.

The leaders who had defeated the French and

who now ruled the new island nation of Haiti considered the remaining Maroons a threat to their power. So they continued to persecute them. In time, the Maroons found that their only defense was to become even more secretive than before. Over the course of many decades, the secret Maroon organizations evolved into secret societies that spread across the Haitian countryside. They became known as the *bizango*, a name that came from the Bissago, a West African tribe. Baron Samedi, who guarded

During the 1791 slave revolt, Haitian leader Toussaint L'Ouverture switched his allegiance to the French in hopes that they would allow blacks to rule the colony.

the dead, became one of their most revered loa. Oaths of secrecy continued to protect the bizango as sons, daughters, and other relatives of members became members themselves.

To discourage people from joining these societies, the government claimed the bizango performed evil rites. Government officials spread rumors about bizango members becoming animals and killing innocent people. After a while, the secret societies actually reinforced these rumors because they gave the groups a strong, fearsome image.

For Justice or Money

The bizango societies began to exercise power over the peasants in the countryside. The primary goal of this power was to do good, to maintain order, and to render justice when the official authorities could or would not do so. For example, if a person committed a crime against a family member or friend, the wronged party could complain to a local bizango. The society would then meet and decide whether to condemn the wrongdoer. If condemned, the wrongdoer received a punishment. The secret societies wanted to strike fear into the hearts of those who threatened the order of Haitian society. So these societies developed severe and frightening punishments.

One punishment was even worse than death in the eyes of Haitians. This was zombification. For many years, according to Wade Davis, the houngans of the bizango had experimented with and perfected the poisons and drugs passed on by the slaves and Maroons. They learned to make a condemned person a zombie. In this way, they removed the wrongdoer from society and forced him or her to serve it by doing forced labor. Bokors, who dealt in the mysteries of dark, left-handed Voodoo, also created zombies. But, while the houngans of the bizango did it for justice, the bokors did it for money.

The secret bizango societies in modern Haiti are the direct descendants of the Maroon bands that formed in the 1700s. They constitute, in effect, a second, "shadow" government coexisting with the island's official government. The bizangos are far too powerful to be eradicated or even successfully harassed by the official authorities. So, because there is no other choice, the authorities tolerate the bizango. These secret groups, by their own design, remain mysterious, almost mythical. Many of their practices have become legendary. Houngans, bokors, and bizango leaders know that zombies are not really dead people brought back to life. Though they truly believe that the magic of religious chants plays some part in zombification, they know that zombie victims are drugged. Many Haitian peasants, however, conditioned by nearly two centuries

Black soldiers in Haiti fight French colonial soldiers during the great revolt of August 1791. The former slaves finally succeeded in driving out the Europeans in 1803.

of fear, continue to believe the legends. For them, zombies are literally the walking dead.

After gaining an understanding of the evolution and social function of the bizango, researchers better understood cases like that of Clairvius Narcisse. For years, Narcisse had treated his relatives and neighbors with disrespect and finally cheated his brother in a land dispute. The brother went to the local bizango seeking justice. Unbeknownst to Narcisse, the bizango found him guilty and condemned him to zombification. He underwent this terrifying process and served in the fields for two years. When his master was killed, Narcisse no longer received the regular doses of the drug that kept him under control. The drug wore off. Although the poison and drugs had done some permanent damage, he regained most of his memory and other normal functions and reentered society. Thus, through scientific and historical research, modern scholars confirmed the existence of zombies. Yet they exploded the myth that the dead in Haiti can walk.

The Mysteries of Voodoo

Scientists have not been so successful, however, in explaining away some of the other mysteries of Voodoo. Chief among these mysteries is a person being possessed by a spirit. The object of most Voodoo rituals is possession. The people want the loa to be present so that they can ask for advice or for intercession with the Gran Mét. The loa becomes accessible to the community when it takes over the body of one of the ritual participants. Many nonbelievers think Voodoo ceremonial possessions must be phony. Yet researchers who have observed Voodoo ceremonies insist that the people undergoing possession do not act in a normal way. As described earlier, they often exhibit unusual strength, are not burned by contact with hot coals, and undergo dramatic voice changes.

In the early 1900s, American and British ob-

This drawing represents a typical Bizango temple altar. The items on the altar include a cross bound with cord and cloths, bottles of rum for offerings, and icons of Christian saints.

servers tried to explain away this voice change as ventriloquism. They claimed the houngan or mambo, not a spirit, actually did the talking. According to this explanation, the priest stood in the shadows or in another room and projected his or her voice into the middle of the hounfour. The "possessed" person mouthed the words, making it appear that a spirit was speaking. Later researchers rejected this idea, since it did not explain how the priest could create a voice completely different from his or her own.

A Powerful Drug

Modern anthropologists and other researchers do not believe Voodoo possession can be explained as trickery. They accept that the people involved in the ceremony believe strongly that an actual possession is taking place. Some psychologists, such as Dr. E. Fuller Torrey, have suggested that possession is accomplished through the power of suggestion. This is a mental process in which a person believes so strongly in an idea that it becomes real in his or her mind. According to Torrey, the one who is about to undergo possession accepts completely that his or her body will temporarily house a spirit. The act of working oneself into a frenzy then becomes a form of self-hypnosis. The man or woman eventually clears the conscious mind of all normal thoughts, inducing a trancelike state. Now, the possessed person plays the role of the spirit, basing the personality details on models already accepted by society. In other words, everyone taking part in the ceremony knows that Ogoun is male and very strong and aggressive. Therefore, the person possessed by Ogoun appropriately uses a male voice and exhibits aggressive behavior. Torrey emphasizes that the possessed person is not aware that he or she is creating the personality out of his or her own mind.

There *are* scientific precedents for the human

"That the peculiar symptoms described by Clairvius Narcisse so closely matched the quite particular symptoms of tetrodotoxin poisoning suggested that he had been exposed to the poison."

Wade Davis, *The Serpent and the Rainbow*

"The widely circulated claim . . . to the effect that tetrodotoxin is the causal agent in the initial zombification process is without factual foundation."

Pharmacologists C.Y. Kao and Takeshi Yasumoto, *Science*, April 1988

A woman writhes wildly as she is possessed by the loa invoked at a Voodoo ceremony. Possession by the spirit is the goal of most Voodoo rituals.

mind creating completely new personalities. The best-known cases are those of people exhibiting multiple personalities. One celebrated and documented case was depicted in the popular film *The Three Faces of Eve*. In addition to her own personality, Eve had two other and very different selves which surfaced from time to time. When one of the other two selves was in control, the woman's normal personality was completely submerged and unaware of what was happening. Psychologists like

Torrey do not suggest that Voodoo possession is caused by multiple personalities. This condition is a rare and serious form of mental illness. However, some researchers feel that similar mental processes and abilities, utilized in some unknown way, may be at work in Voodoo possession.

Unexplainable Experiences

Although psychological theories appear to explain some of the mysteries of Voodoo possession, they do not explain all of them. Some researchers have pointed out that even people with multiple personalities cannot change their voices as completely as do many who undergo possession. And powers of the mind do not account for people doubling and tripling their strength or displaying immunity to hot coals. These things remain unexplained.

Perhaps science will someday provide conclusive evidence explaining the mysteries of Voodoo. Even if this happens, it is unlikely that believers will change their minds. For them, as well as for members of other religions, the acceptance of strange and supernatural happenings will undoubtedly remain a matter of faith. By its very definition, faith involves accepting something in the absence of supporting evidence. From a scientific standpoint, this is not logical. But it is part of human nature that what people believe in their hearts to be real often resists and defies the arguments of logic.

Five

Voodoo in the United States

Voodoo first arrived in the United States in the eighteenth century in the area of New Orleans, Louisiana. During the 1700s and early 1800s, the Spanish, and later the French, ruled Louisiana. They imported slaves to work on farms and sugar and cotton plantations. These slaves came not only from Africa, but also from some of the Caribbean islands. The slaves who came directly from Africa practiced the Yoruba faith or other faiths of western Africa. Those from the Caribbean introduced various offshoots of Voodoo, including Trinidadian Shango, to the southern United States. Shortly after Louisiana became a U.S. territory in 1803, many free immigrants from Haiti traveled to New Orleans looking for work. They brought Haitian Voodoo practices to the area. All of these various yet related faiths came together in Louisiana and over the course of time evolved into a unique American version of Voodoo, often referred to as New Orleans Voodoo.

An Emphasis on Magic

Some people still practice New Orleans Voodoo in Louisiana and other parts of the southern United States. But this form of worship reached its height of popularity in the nineteenth century. New Or-

leans Voodoo carried on many of the traditions and customs of Haitian Voodoo. These included many of the same gods, spirits, ceremonies, and chants familiar to Haitians. However, the emphasis and flavor of Voodoo changed in Louisiana.

In New Orleans, the most important religious figures were women. The reason for this remains unclear. These female priests, often referred to as Voodoo queens, were highly respected and sometimes even feared by Voodoo worshippers. The most famous of these Voodoo queens was Marie Laveau, who practiced her magic in the mid-1800s. Usually, she created magic for a fee. Many people loved and admired her because, they believed, she could use her powers to do good. Others feared her, believing she could also do evil things such as drive someone insane or even kill a person. Still others thought that Laveau was a fake who took advantage of people's belief in Voodoo to make money. Marie Laveau remains a controversial figure in Louisiana history.

Dambala

Another way Voodoo changed in the United States was that one particular loa became more important than any other. This was Dambala, associated primarily with snakes. Many special ceremonies honored Dambala, and snakes became special symbols in the lives and ceremonies of believers. Often, for instance, female priests wore headdresses adorned with the likenesses of snakes.

Perhaps the most important difference was that New Orleans Voodoo placed much more emphasis on magic and especially the elements of left-handed Voodoo—evil magic. In Haiti, left-handed Voodoo was not part of the mainstream of Voodoo worship. In New Orleans, by contrast, the power of magic— both good and evil—became far more important and accepted. Magic practiced for constructive purposes, such as healing or bringing good luck, be-

Nineteenth-century New Orleans Voodoo queen Marie Laveau crouches in a chair while her assistant stands close by. Although the controversial Laveau is represented here as a malevolent hag, many people believed her to be good.

came known as white magic. Magic that brought bad luck or even death to someone became known as black magic.

Jujus and Mojos

White magic was much more important and widespread in New Orleans Voodoo than black magic. This was because most believers were more interested in bringing themselves or loved ones good luck than in hurting others. Most people avoided resorting to black magic since those same evil powers might later be turned on them. One of the most important symbols in white magic was the *juju*, or good luck charm. There were many well-known jujus, some meant to be worn around the neck or carried in a pocket. The most common were rabbits' feet, chickens' feet, and the paws of monkeys. Other jujus supposedly brought good luck when people placed them above their doors. For example, believers held that nailing a straw broom over the door would help ward off disease. A dried alligator head or horseshoe hung above a door was also said to bring good luck.

Another element of white magic was the good hex. A hex was a magic spell intentionally cast to bring either good or bad luck. A common use of a good hex was to bring a person good luck in a romantic relationship. Or a good hex might be used to make crops grow better or to help clear the name of a person wrongly accused of a crime.

People also used hexes in performing black magic. A bad luck hex, called a *mojo*, was a curse. According to believers, someone could use a mojo to scare people, bring them some kind of misfortune, or even kill them. Some mojos consisted mainly of the spell one person cast over another. But sometimes these curses were accompanied by physical symbols that emphasized the power of evil. For example, after casting a spell, a person might place a tiny black casket on the doorstep of the victim. This marked the victim for misfortune or death within a certain length of time. Voodoo dolls were another form of symbolic mojo. Supposedly, sticking pins into a doll representing the victim reinforced the spell already cast.

Making the Magic

In New Orleans Voodoo, both white and black magic were important aspects of Voodoo worship. The various spells cast sought the power, approval, or blessing of a known spirit. According to believers, the most powerful magic, white or black, came from a Voodoo queen. However, anyone could perform magic if he or she knew the right prayer

A Voodoo doll is a type of symbolic mojo, or evil spell. A physical representation of a person and the use of the pins are believed to strengthen and direct the curse.

chants, or "conjures," and had access to certain essential materials. These usually included specific herbs, spices, animal parts, human bones, and various types of soil and dirt. The person combined the appropriate materials in a "recipe" for the desired magic. Sometimes, people placed these mixtures in small bags known as *gris-gris*. This term comes from French and means "gray-gray." Since gray is a combination of white and black, the term gris-gris symbolized the fact that magic Voodoo recipes could be used in either white or black magic. When used in white magic, a gris-gris might be hung on a wall or above a door. In black magic, a person sometimes placed a gris-gris on the victim's doorstep. In this case, the gris-gris was used as a

Al Petschonek, owner of the Alchemist Shop in St. Louis, Missouri, follows an ancient recipe to mix a magic brew. Petschonek believes potions and amulets are simply instruments to conduct spiritual power, not the source of the power itself.

symbolic mojo, a warning to the victim.

The recipes used to create Voodoo magic were many, varied, and extremely colorful. Believers in the United States passed these recipes from one generation to another. And worshipers often invented new recipes to supplement the old. In her book *Jambalaya*, Luisah Teish has compiled many recipes, both old and new, for white magic. Teish, a writer and practitioner of New Orleans-style Voodoo, describes personal ceremonies and magic recipes which, she says, people can use in their everyday life. For example, Teish recommends a charm to stop gossip. The ingredients: salt, a whole beef tongue, black pepper, a spool of black cord, a piece of unused parchment paper, a fountain pen, Dragon's Blood ink, nine steel pins, a whip or leather belt, and a piece of black cloth. Teish lists the following steps:

1. Split a cheap beef tongue in half, beginning at the base (wide end). Leave the tip intact.

2. Write the name of the gossiper on the unused parchment: "May the wagging tongue of (name) burn till bitter turns to sweet." (If you do not know the name, simply use "the wagging tongue.")

3. Lay the paper lengthwise in the center of the tongue and cover the entire center with black paper.

4. Close the tongue and fasten seams with the steel pins. Put four pins on each side, and pierce the tip with the ninth pin.

5. Wrap the tongue from base to tip in black cord. Wrap it tightly.

6. Place the tongue on a piece of black cloth and put it in a dark closet or under a piece of furniture.

7. Rise every morning at 6 A.M. and whip the tongue with the leather strap. Think of the disharmony caused by the gossip as you beat the tongue. Do this every day until the tongue begins to smell of decay.

8. Then cover the tongue with salt and wrap it in the black cloth.

9. Take the tongue for a ride to a large body of water. As you throw the tongue in the ocean, lake, or river, say, "May his/her mouth be cleaned." Return home by a different route. Wash your hands with salt and water and eat a piece of something sweet.

There are also recipes for black magic, although they are not as easily found as those for white magic.

Is Black Magic Real?

Are the hexes of black magic real? Can people use magic to make others die or go insane? Many stories tell of incidents in which these things happened. But nonbelievers, especially scientists, try to explain these events in logical ways. For example, some researchers have offered scientific explanations for the well-known case of New Orleans businessman J.B. Langrast. In the 1850s, Langrast publicly denounced legendary Voodoo queen Marie Laveau and blamed several robberies and murders on her followers. Soon, gris-gris containing roosters' heads began appearing on Langrast's doorstep. He became increasingly agitated and eventually blasted his front steps with a shotgun. Afterward, he fled New Orleans, leaving behind his relatives and a considerable fortune.

Was Langrast a victim of Voodoo black magic? According to Voodoo believers, Marie Laveau caused Langrast to go insane. Supposedly, she asked a loa to curse him with madness, and the spirit had channeled its powers through the gris-gris. But most nonbelievers do not accept this explanation. They insist that there is no direct evidence that Marie Laveau's mojo actually caused Langrast's insanity. In fact, they say, it has never even been proven that the man *was* insane. Some

A woman visits the tomb of Marie Laveau. The marker says Laveau died June 11, 1897, at the age of sixty-two and asks passers-by to pray for her. The X's inscribed on the marker by visitors probably have a magical purpose.

This New York City shop, called a botanica, carries articles needed by followers of Santeria, a Voodoo-style religion brought to the United States from Cuba. A wide variety of herbs, herbal oils, and brews used in Santeria are available here. Note the shrine with statue, candles, and plate with monetary offerings at the left of the photo.

people conclude that Langrast's irrational actions, including leaving town, were prompted by fear. He believed Marie Laveau's followers might kill him if he stayed.

Some psychologists, such as E. Fuller Torrey, theorize that it was Langrast's own mind, not Marie Laveau's spells, that did the damage. As in the case of Voodoo possession, the power of suggestion may have been at work in Langrast's case. If so, it did not matter that he claimed not to believe in Voodoo magic. His subconscious, or inner mind, believed

"Who has been stuffing our contemporaries in the matter of the defunct Voudou queen, Marie Lavoux [sic]? For they have undoubtedly been stuffed, nay crammed, by some huge practical joker."

H.J. Hearsay, editor, *New Orleans Democrat*, 1881

"In Haiti [Marie Laveau] would have been considered a mediocre priestess, but here she was a remarkable person, who gave the people what they wanted."

Raymond J. Martinez, *Mysterious Marie Laveau, Voodoo Priestess*

that such magic might be possible. It was this hidden belief that slowly convinced him that Laveau's powers were working. Perhaps then, in a sense, Langrast drove himself insane!

Some psychologists suggest that Voodoo death, or death caused by black magic, might also be the result of the power of suggestion. In such a case, the victim may accept the reality of his or her impending death. In some cases, the victim's relatives may also accept his or her approaching death and treat the victim as though he or she has already left the land of the living. After days or weeks, the victim may die as the result of neglect, depression, and despair. Does the power of suggestion explain the weird phenomena of Voodoo black magic? Or are these strange happenings caused by the wrath of the loa as believers claim? Unfortunately, there is no way to be sure which explanation is correct. For the time being, Marie Laveau's powers and the practice of Voodoo black magic remain mysterious and unexplained.

Spirit Worship

In addition to New Orleans-style Voodoo, people practice other kinds of Voodoo in the United States. Of these, Santeria is the most widespread. Santeria, which originated in Cuba in the 1800s, has the same roots as Haitian Voodoo. The Spanish brought West African slaves to Cuba to work on sugar plantations, and the slaves carried their Yoruba religious traditions with them. In Cuba, these traditions fused with Christian ideas and symbols as they did in Haiti. The Cuban slaves developed a syncretic faith similar to Haitian Voodoo.

In 1959, the military and political revolution led by Fidel Castro forced many Cubans to flee their country. Most of those who left went to Puerto Rico, Venezuela, and the United States. In the United States, large Cuban communities developed in Miami, New York City, Newark, Detroit, Chicago, and several smaller cities. The number of people who practice Santeria in these cities is unknown. But the rapid spread of the religion can be seen by the number of botanicas that have opened in the last thirty years. These are small retail stores that sell herbs and other materials used in Santeria ceremonies. In 1990, there were more than 100 botanicas in Miami and at least 120 in New York City.

Santeria, like Haitian Voodoo, is mainly concerned with the worship of spirits. Believers in Santeria have retained the Yoruba term *orisha* to describe the spirits. Many other Yoruba terms are still used, including the name for priests, *babalawos*, and the names of gods such as Obatala. Also like Haitian Voodoo, Santeria associates various Yoruba

Cuban refugees fleeing Castro's communist takeover in 1959 arrive in New York City to start new lives. Many Cuban refugees brought Santeria beliefs and practices with them to the United States.

A Cuban woman in New York City prepares an altar for a Santeria service. The sacrificing of animals in this cult has disturbed some nonbelieving New Yorkers.

spirits with corresponding Christian saints. For example, Orunmila, the spirit who foretells religious events, is linked to Saint Francis of Assisi. Santeria ceremonies are very much like those in Haiti. There are feasts, drums, and wild dances leading up to possession of members of the congregation by spirits. In Santeria, a spirit "descends" and "seizes the head" of the person being possessed. Animal sacrifices appease the hunger of the orisha. Chickens are the most common animals sacrificed, and the slaughter is accomplished quickly, cleanly, and humanely with modern equipment. After a sacrifice, the worshipers cook and eat the animals as part of the offering to the orisha.

While Santeria has much in common with other forms of Voodoo, it also has some important differences. For example, there are no zombies in Santeria as there are in Haitian Voodoo. And there is much less emphasis in Santeria on magic spells than there is in New Orleans Voodoo. In the latter, herbs are used mainly in recipes for hexes. In San-

Votive candles, statues, and crucifixes are sold in this botanica. Prescriptions for the magical uses of such items are posted above them.

Dr. Charles Wetli, a Dade County, Florida, assistant medical examiner, displays human skulls and bones confiscated by police from a Santeria cult in Miami. The cult flourishes in south Florida, which has a large Cuban community.

teria, by contrast, herbs are used primarily to cleanse, refresh, and prepare worshipers for contact with and possession by the orisha.

The Gift of Prophecy

One of the most important elements of Santeria is the gift of prophecy. This is the ability to foresee the future. According to believers, during possession a person receives the gift of prophecy from an orisha. Usually, this power is only temporary but remains long enough for the person to foretell one or more future events. Most often, the things predicted concern the lives of the individuals in the local community. Those gifted with the ability of prophecy often predict marriages, births, periods of good or bad fortune, illnesses, and deaths.

Practitioners of Santeria believe the gift of

prophecy can sometimes be used to prevent bad future events. By performing the right ritual, their petition to the orisha for protection may be answered. One documented case occurred in the 1970s. Anthropologist Migene Gonzalez-Whippler was studying American Santeria. She attended a ceremony in which the worshipers sacrificed a chicken and later ate it. According to the babalawo, they did this to protect Gonzalez-Whippler from danger that lurked in her future. Now, the worshipers claimed, an orisha protected her.

Several weeks later, Gonzalez-Whippler took an airplane from Denmark to the United States. During the flight, the plane experienced serious engine trouble and had to turn back. Worried the plane might crash, Danish officials cleared the runways and called for emergency equipment. Luckily, the

Ysamur Flores Pena, a Los Angeles Santeria priest, or babalawo, poses in front of an altar honoring his ancestors. Pena and other Santeria adherents claim the U.S. Bill of Rights grants them the freedom to worship in their own way—including the sacrifice of animals. Animal rights activists disagree.

plane landed safely. According to Santeria believers, the anthropologist survived because of the protection of the orisha. Gonzalez-Whippler agreed, saying, "I believe quite strongly, that . . . the blood of the chicken saved me and more than three hundred other people from almost certain death."

Skeptics suggest that Gonzalez-Whippler's near brush with death had nothing to do with orishas and sacrificed chickens. They insist the incident was nothing more than coincidence. According to this view, just as many protected people die in accidents as do unprotected people. However, the ones who survive receive much recognition and publicity from believers, while those who die do not. This gives the false impression that most people pro-

In Miami, a botanica owner is surrounded by a mystifying assortment of dolls, beaded jewelry, horse tails and shoes, plants, and hand-carved bowls. In many parts of the United States, interest in the occult continues to grow.

tected by an orisha survive misfortune.

Despite such arguments that seek to explain away the mysteries of Santeria, believers remain true to their faith. They continue to pray and sacrifice, secure in their feelings that the spirits are listening to and watching over them. They see Santeria as a positive and very workable religion that should be respected just like Christianity and other religions. They recognize that part of the skepticism expressed by doubters is due to a lack of understanding and respect for Santeria by many Americans. In fact, few Americans are familiar with Santeria and its beliefs, and many who do know of the faith find its practices strange. But this, some believers say, will change as the religion spreads. As Cuban communities in the United States grow larger and expand into other cities, the practice of Santeria in the United States will become more widespread. In time, more and more Americans will be exposed to the belief system of Santeria. Followers of the faith hope that such exposure will eventually lead to understanding and respect.

"These [Santeria claims] are mysteries, but that's not to say they won't be explained. I think in the future, scientists will write a formula for these things."

John Amira, Santeria drummer, *New York*, October 12, 1987

"No person's life or culture is, in the final analysis, logical."

Karen McCarthy Brown, *Mama Lola*

Epilogue

The Search Goes On

Followers of Voodoo, both in the Caribbean and in the United States, accept such supernatural elements as spirit possession and magic as mysterious yet real. In contrast, many scientists and other skeptics assume that these mysteries have logical, though still unknown, explanations. Which view is correct? That of the worshipers or that of the skeptics? No one knows for sure.

Skeptics say belief in the supernatural is irrational because no evidence supports it. Many will continue to search for rational answers to religious mysteries, including those of Voodoo. They will seek measurable, weighable evidence to support their theories. But believers doubt such theories will ever be proven. They say religion has always been a matter of faith rather than evidence. Believers will continue to accept the mysteries of religion as the work of spirits or the will of God.

The fact is that people do not worship God because it is rational or logical to do so. Instead, their belief comes from their hearts. No amount of scientific explanation can dissuade a religious person from believing the supernatural tenets of his or her faith. The mystical stories, ideas, and practices of Voodoo and other faiths may be hard for nonbeliev-

ers to accept. But to believers they are the miracles that make their faiths special. Writer Joseph M. Murphy echoed the devotion felt by followers of every faith when he said of Santeria, "It is a miracle because it is true."

Spectators at a Voodoo ceremony in Rio de Janeiro clap their hands in time with the beat of a drum as they watch a ritual unfold. Brazil's government says that less than 1 percent of the country's population prefers Voodoo-style religions to mainstream Roman Catholicism. Voodoo leaders claim that the number is around 10 percent.

Glossary

anesthetic: A substance that induces numbness or loss of consciousness, most often used in surgery.

anthropology: The scientific study of the origins, cultures, and religious practices of human beings.

asson: In Voodoo ceremonies, a rattle used to alert the spirits.

babalawo: A priest in the Yoruba and Santeria religions.

bizango: In Haiti, secret societies that constitute a second, "shadow" government of the country.

bokor: In Haiti, a sorcerer who does magic in return for money.

botanica: A small retail store that sells herbs and other materials used in the practice of Santeria.

communion: In Catholicism, a ceremony in which worshipers drink wine representing Christ's blood and eat wafers representing Christ's body.

conjure: A prayer chant in New Orleans Voodoo.

curare: A powerful plant poison used as an anesthetic.

gede: Festive Voodoo spirits honored in October during the Feast of All Souls.

Gine: The ancestral home of the Haitian blacks, referring to Guinea, or Africa.

Gran Mèt: The Almighty Master; God.

gris-gris: A small bag containing a recipe for magic in New Orleans Voodoo.

gros bon ange: In Voodoo, part of the soul, a life force shared by all people.

hex: A magic spell in New Orleans Voodoo.

hounfour: In Haiti, the religious temple where Voodoo ceremonies take place.

houngan: A male priest in Haitian Voodoo.

hounsis: Initiates, or helpers, in a Voodoo temple.

juju: A good luck charm in New Orleans Voodoo.

left-handed Voodoo: The darker side of Voodoo, concerned with evil, black magic, and/or zombies.

loa: The spirits in Haitian Voodoo.

mambo: A female priest in Haitian Voodoo.

Maroons: In Haitian history, runaway slaves who had their own secret communities in the hills.

mèt tet: "Masters of the head," one's personal guiding spirit.

mojo: A bad luck hex, or curse, in New Orleans Voodoo.

n'âme: In Voodoo, the quality of the flesh that keeps individual cells and body parts functioning.

Obeah: The Voodoolike religion practiced on the Caribbean island of Jamaica.

orisa (orisha): The spirit in the Yoruba faith, and also in Santeria.

Saint Domingue: The French Caribbean colony of the 1600s and 1700s that later became Haiti.

Santeria: The Voodoolike religion of Cuba that spread to the United States in the twentieth century.

Shango: The Voodoolike religion practiced on the Caribbean island of Trinidad.

syncretic faith: A religion formed by uniting ideas from two or more faiths.

tetrodotoxin: A deadly poison found in some types of puffer fish.

ti bon ange: In Voodoo, the part of the soul that contains the personality and other unique personal traits.

vévé: In Voodoo ceremonies, a special design made with flour or ashes to summon a spirit.

Voodoo: The religion of Haiti, as well as other Caribbean islands and parts of the southern United States.

Yoruba: A people inhabiting parts of western Africa.

zombie astral: In Haitian legend, a part of the soul captured by a sorcerer and made to do the sorcerer's bidding.

zombie cadavre: In Haitian legend, a soulless dead person who walks among the living.

zombification: The process of turning a person into a zombie.

Bibliography

Sandra T. Barnes, ed., *Africa's Ogun: Old World and New.* Bloomington: Indiana University Press, 1989.

William Booth, "Voodoo Science," *Science*, April 15, 1988.

Karen McCarthy Brown, *Mama Lola: A Voodoo Priestess in Brooklyn.* Berkeley: University of California Press, 1991.

Barbara Christensen, *The Magic and Meaning of Voodoo.* Milwaukee: Raintree Books, 1977.

Nancy Cooper, "Haiti's Voodoo Witch Hunt: Settling Old Scores Against Houngan and Mambos," *Newsweek*, May 26, 1986.

Wade Davis, *The Serpent and the Rainbow.* New York: Warner Books, 1985.

Carole Devillers, "Haiti's Voodoo Pilgrimages of Spirits and Saints," *National Geographic*, March 1985.

Harry Eastwell, "Voodoo Death and the Mechanism for Dispatch of the Dying in East Arnhem, Australia," *American Anthropologist,* vol. 84, no. 1.

Encyclopedia of World Religions. London: Octopus, 1975.

Charles Massicot Gandolfo, *Voodoo in South Louisiana.* New Orleans: The New Orleans

Historic Voodoo Musuem, 1987.

Migene Gonzalez-Whippler, *Santeria: The Religion.* New York: Harmony Books, 1989.

Migene Gonzalez-Whippler, *The Santeria Experience.* Englewood Cliffs, NJ: Prentice-Hall, 1982.

Marvin Harris, "Death by Voodoo," *Psychology Today*, August 1984.

Jim Haskins, *Voodoo & Hoodoo: Their Tradition and Craft as Revealed by Actual Practitioners.* Chelsea, MI: Scarborough House, 1990.

Nick Jordan, "What's in a Zombie?" *Psychology Today,* May 1984.

Susan Katz, "A Pantheon of Spirits," *Newsweek*, February 24, 1986.

Raymond J. Martinez, *Mysterious Marie Laveau.* New Orleans: Hope Publications, 1956.

Alfred Métraux, *Voodoo in Haiti.* New York: Schocken Books, 1959.

Joseph M. Murphy, *Santeria: An African Religion in America.* Boston: Beacon Books, 1988.

Milo Rigaud, *Secrets of Voodoo.* San Francisco: City Lights Books, 1985.

Louis Saas, "Voodoo Therapy," *Vogue*, September 1986.

Luisah Teish, *Jambalaya.* New York: Harper & Row, 1985.

E. Fuller Torrey, *Witchdoctors and Psychiatrists: The Common Roots of Psychotherapy and Its Future.* New York: Harper & Row, 1986.

Joseph J. Williams, *Voodoos and Obeahs.* New York: AMS Press, 1932.

Index

About the Authors

Don Nardo is an actor, film director, composer, and award-winning author. He has appeared in more than fifty stage productions and has worked before or behind the camera in twenty films. Several of his musical compositions, including a young person's version of *The War of the Worlds* and the oratorio *Richard III*, have been played by regional orchestras. Mr. Nardo's writing credits include short stories, articles, and more than twenty-five books, including *Lasers: Humanity's Magic Light, Anxiety and Phobias, The Irish Potato Famine, Gravity: The Universal Force,* and *The Mexican-American War.* Among his other writings are an episode of ABC Television's "Spenser: For Hire" and numerous screenplays. Mr. Nardo lives with his wife, Christine, on Cape Cod, Massachusetts.

Erik Belgum is a graduate of the University of Minnesota and has done additional study at the Eastman School of Music and the MacPhail School of Music. He is a free-lance writer and musical composer with special interests in fiction, computers, and electronic music. His writing credits include short stories, nonfiction articles, and musical compositions. He is the author of *Artificial Intelligence: Opposing Viewpoints. Voodoo: Opposing Viewpoints* is his second book in the Great Mysteries series.

Picture Credits

AP/Wide World Photos, 26, 29, 32, 91, 94, 95, 96
The Bettmann Archive, 41, 66, 72, 77
Doré Bible Illustrations/Dover Publications, 24
Frost Publishing Group, 25
Historic New Orleans Collection, 23, 85, 87, 90
Library of Congress, 74
Brian McGovern, 10, 14, 16, 20, 22, 36, 38, 43, 44, 47, 51, 57, 61, 64, 80
Benjamin Montag, 27, 35, 55, 78
Reuters/Bettmann, 97
UPI/Bettmann, 9, 13, 30, 40, 49, 69, 83, 88, 93, 101